Awards, Publication Acknowledgments
& American Editions of
# Where Lightning Strikes

Awards

• The Isabel & Mary Neff Fellowship for Creative Writing (University of Cincinnati) 1984-1985

• Elliston Poetry Prize, First Place (anonymous competition; University of Cincinnati) 1985

• Elliston Poetry Prize, Second Place (anonymous competition; University of Cincinnati) 1984

• Elliston Poetry Prize, Grand Prize (no other prize awarded) (anonymous competition; University of Cincinnati) 1983

Publication Acknowledgments

Portions of *Where Lightning Strikes* have appeared previously (sometimes in altered form or under different titles, and under the name "Sherri" Szeman) in the following publications:

Journals

• *Black Warrior Review* (University of Alabama)
• *Centennial Review* (Michigan State University)
• *Chicago Review* (University of Chicago)
• *Colorado-North Review* (University of Northern Colorado)
• *Cornfield Review* (Ohio State University at Marion)
• *Dark Horse*

- *Jeopardy* (Western Washington University)
- *Jewish Currents*
- *The Kenyon Review* (Kenyon College)
- *Literary Review* (Fairleigh Dickinson University)
- *MSS* (State University of New York)
- *Nebo* (Arkansas Technical University)
- *New Kent Quarterly* (Kent State University)
- *Ohio Journal* (Ohio State University)
- *Red Cedar Review* (Michigan State University)
- *Sidewinder* (Texas College of the Mainland)
- *Wisconsin Review* (University of Wisconsin Oshkosh)
- *Writers' Forum* (University of Colorado at Colorado Springs)

Books

- *Survivor: One Who Survives* (Ph.D. dissertation, original poetry, University of Cincinnati) 1986

About
Where Lightning Strikes
(award-winning poems on the Holocaust)

Where Lightning Strikes includes all Szeman's Holocaust poetry, from the poems featured in her Ph.D. dissertation *Survivor: One Who Survives,* to the original versions of "Rachel's poems" appearing or mentioned in Szeman's award-winning, critically acclaimed first novel *The Kommandant's Mistress.*

The poems in this collection revisit the classic themes that have inspired poets for generations: love, passion, betrayal, doubt, loyalty, despair, faith, and survival — this time in the context of the period before, during, and after the Holocaust with its systematic persecution and extermination of the majority of European Jewry by the Nazi regime.

In this collection, victims are given voices. In "First Day of German Class" a young, teenaged girl unfamiliar with the Nazis and their atrocities in Germany and other Nazi-occupied territory develops a crush on the handsome and enigmatic SS Officer who passes out the yellow Stars of David they must now wear, like a brand, to identify and isolate them from the rest of the population.

In the author's first Holocaust poem, "Cutthroat: A Player Who Plays for Himself" — excerpted in *The Kommandant's Mistress* — a female inmate forced into sexual servitude by the Kommandant of the camp considers suicide as an escape from her personal bondage and from the camp, even as she alternately pities or condemns those "weak enough" to "go to the wire" (grab the electric fence), offering her own suggestions for suicide to "escape" the intolerable situation.

"Survivor: One Who Survives," the title poem of Szeman's dissertation, also mentioned in her first novel as one of Rachel's poems/books, explores the life of a woman who "survived" her experiences in the camps but is having difficulty "living."

Other disturbing yet fascinating poems trace the Holocaust from the perpetrators' perspective. We hear Albert Speer's musings about which "path" to take in the dramatic monologue "Learning the New Language," in which he initially claims not to understand the "new language" that everyone in the Nazi-regime is speaking, but then begins to practice some of the words himself.

A Warsaw Ghetto guard in "The Dead Bodies That Line The Streets" bitterly complains about all the dead bodies who watch his every movement, whisper behind his back, and generally prevent him from doing his job effectively and from sleeping well.

Early, unnamed versions of Max (of *The Kommandant's Mistress*) appear, isolated and morally confused in "Dead: Out of Play Though Not Necessarily Out of the Game," where he momentarily sees an inmate as a fellow human being.

A younger SS officer finds himself disconcerted and alarmed after he is unexpectedly attracted to one of the female inmates when he sees her dancing ballet to the music floating from his office window in "White on White."

In the camp itself, one of the *Sonderkommando,* who were in charge of guiding the Jews to be exterminated into the gas chambers, gives "instructions" to a new member of this chosen group on how to survive the camp, in the grim yet spiritually philosophical "On the Other Hand." Nursery rhymes and children's songs take on a deadly, mesmerizing meaning in the stunning, award-winning "Lager-Lieder (Camp Songs)."

The true story of Auschwitz-survivor Anna Brunn Ornstein, who was in the camp as a young girl with her mother, is transformed from Anna's own stories and related in the haunting yet moving poem "Sofie and Anna."

Haunting depictions of abusers' and survivors' lives after the war appear in works like "Those Who Claim We Hated Them," where the narrator insists — not always convincingly — that he, his family, and his colleagues held no contempt whatsoever for the Jews, and only did what was politically and morally required of them so that they themselves might survive the Nazi regime and the War.

In the collection's title work, "Where Lightning Strikes," a survivor of the camps who now holds a Professorship likens his encounter with contemporary anti-Semitism to a tree's being struck by lightning: swift, unexpected, brutal, devastating, but terrifyingly and sadly illuminating.

Szeman's work speaks to us with clarity and resonance. Her themes, though set, in this collection, around the Holocaust, are universal, encompassing the perpetrators', victims', and survivors' perspectives equally insightfully. Though the line-breaks are syllabic — imitating the arbitrary rigidity of the Nazi persecutions as well as of the concentration camps' operations — the language flows passionately over the artificially imposed line-breaks and formal stanzas. The poems' many fans often state that, despite the fact that they may have been initially wary of the subject matter, they were enthralled and shaken by poetry which so clearly, simply, and memorably portrays such complex and harrowing events in human history.

All of the poems in this collection have been previously published in literary and university journals, and many of the poems in this collection have been awarded prizes, including the University of Cincinnati's Elliston Prize (anonymous competition; 1983, 1984, 1985), Michigan State University's *The Centennial Review* Michael Miller Award for Poetry (1985), and The Isabel & Mary Neff Fellowship for Creative Writing (1984-85). Several poems were part of her dissertation, *Survivor: One Who Survives* (University of Cincinnati, 1986). Along with her non-Holocaust poetry collection, *Love in the Time of Dinosaurs,* this volume, *Where Lightning Strikes,* was unanimously accepted for publication by all outside readers of UKA Press in 2004.

As powerful, unsettling, and lyrical as her first novel, *The Kommandant's Mistress,* these poems will take you on a compelling, chilling, and unforgettable journey into the lives, hearts, and minds of all those who were victims, perpetrators, and survivors of the Holocaust.

Other Books by
Alexandria Constantinova Szeman

Novels

The Kommandant's Mistress, Revised & Expanded, 20th Anniversary Edition

Only with the Heart, Revised & Expanded, Legally & Medically Updated, 12th Anniversary Edition

No Feet in Heaven

The Kommandant's Mistress (1st Edition: HarperCollins 1993, 5 printings; HarperPerennial 1994, 4 printings; 2nd Edition [with translations of Verdi's opera *La Traviata*]: Arcade 2000, 6 printings), (formerly writing as "Sherri")

Only with the Heart (1st Edition: Arcade 2000, 8 printings), (formerly writing as "Sherri")

Short Stories

Naked, with Glasses

Poetry

Love in the Time of Dinosaurs

Where Lightning Strikes: Poems on the Holocaust

Creative Writing
Non-fiction

Mastering Point of View: Using POV and Fiction Elements to Create Conflict, Develop Characters, Revise Your Work, & Improve Your Craft, Revised, Updated, & Expanded, 12th Anniversary Edition

Mastering Point of View: How to Control POV to Create Conflict, Depth, & Suspense; (Story Press 2001, 4 printings), (formerly writing as "Sherri")

Where Lightning Strikes

award-winning poems
on the Holocaust

Alexandria Constantinova Szeman
(formerly writing as "Sherri")

RWP
RockWay Press, LLC • New Mexico

Permissions & Publication Acknowledgments

Portions of *Where Lightning Strikes* have appeared previously (sometimes in altered form or under different titles, and under the name "Sherri" Szeman) in the following publications:

Journals

- *Black Warrior Review* (University of Alabama)
- *Centennial Review* (Michigan State University)
- *Chicago Review* (University of Chicago)
- *Colorado-North Review* (University of Northern Colorado)
- *Cornfield Review* (Ohio State University at Marion)
- *Dark Horse*
- *Jeopardy* (Western Washington University)
- *Jewish Currents*
- *The Kenyon Review* (Kenyon College)
- *Literary Review* (Fairleigh Dickinson University)
- *MSS* (State University of New York)
- *Nebo* (Arkansas Technical University)
- *New Kent Quarterly* (Kent State University)

- *Ohio Journal* (Ohio State University)
- *Red Cedar Review* (Michigan State University)
- *Sidewinder* (Texas College of the Mainland)
- *Wisconsin Review* (University of Wisconsin Oshkosh)
- *Writers' Forum* (University of Colorado at Colorado Springs)

Books

- *Survivor: One Who Survives* (Ph.D. dissertation, original poetry, University of Cincinnati, 1986)

RockWay Press Trade Paper ISBN 9780977663439
LCCN 2012907385
E-Book ISBN 9780977663491

- Cover Artwork from Author's personal collection of World War II original photographs, Image untitled
- Section divider designed by Francesco Abrignani (collection #12495781), provided by 123RF.com, sister company of Inmaginecom. Used with permission.
- Cover design by Alexandria Szeman & RockWay Press, LLC. Copyright © 2012 Alexandria Szeman & RockWay Press, LLC.
- Interior design by RockWay Press, LLC. Copyright © 2013 Alexandria Szeman & RockWay Press, LLC.
- Author Photograph © 2013 by Alexandria Szeman.

RWP

Visit our Web site at RockWayPress.com

for those who survived
and
for those who did not

Acknowledgments

Grateful acknowledgment is made to the people who have read my poetry faithfully over the years, giving me valuable critiques, suggestions, and feedback. I became a better poet because of your unwavering honesty: Becky Keller, Sharon Brown, Terrence Glass, Christopher Williams, Kelly Wingo, Evelyn Schott, and Barbara Walker. Thank you.

To Auschwitz-survivors Anna and Paul Ornstein, who read my very first Holocaust Poem, "Cutthroat: A Player Who Plays for Himself," and thought that I, too, had been in the concentration camps; and who subsequently not only read every one of my Holocaust poems, but who honored me by sharing their own stories and personal experiences with me. Anna, thank you for sharing the stories of your mother's and your experiences in Auschwitz, which formed the basis of the poem "Sofie and Anna."

To Human Rights Activist and renowned author Elie Wiesel, who survived Auschwitz, Buna, and Buchenwald Concentration Camps; who not only honored me by actually reading the collection of poems I sent him in 1990, but who replied with a handwritten letter complimenting my work (and who didn't take umbrage when I phoned to leave a message of gratitude with his assistant, who wasn't at work that early in the morning, then chastised him for answering his own phone: you were so gracious). I only wish half the people in the world were as good as you, and I treasure the compliments, the hand-written letter you sent an unknown poet, and the fact that you actually spoke to me and talked to me about my poems when I called.

To my German-Jewish great-grandparents, Grandma and Grandpa Hirsch, who tried to protect us from anti-Semitism by not telling anyone we were Jewish (though they honored Sabbath, spoke Yiddish, and never attended Church) and by sending their children, grandchildren, and great-grandchildren to Catholic Schools, where I got called a "Yid" virtually every day. I remember everything you told me, and I always will. This book on the Holocaust, too, is for you.

To my dissertation advisors, Michael Atkinson, Don Bogen, and Tom LeClair, who gave me free reign to explore my own subject matter, styles, and creative growth while working for three years on *Survivor: One Who Survives*. You represent and encouraged the ideal academic environment, fostering independent thinking, originality, and creativity.

To Andrea Lowne, Publisher of UKA [United Kingdom Authors] Press, and to its outside readers & judges — all authors, editors, and publishers themselves — who not only accepted *Where Lightning Strikes,* but unanimously accepted it. Bless you for giving an unknown poet what all poets dream of: an international audience. I am honored to be associated with UKA Press.

I also want to thank Andrea Lowne for allowing me to do the e-book version of *Where Lightning Strikes* before UKA Press was ready to do the Trade Paper edition. Your professional grace and courtesy is part of what makes me honored to have my name associated with your Press.

To Spike, Zoë, Vinnie, Hannah, Zeke, and Mosie: thank you for your unconditional love while you were in our lives. You are in my life and memory forever. To Shooter Tov, Mr. Eli, Trixie, Ling, Sascha, Sophie, and Sadie-Doggie: Thanks for keeping me company when I work.

To Tom, you have my heart, and not just because you read everything I write.

———————————⟫⟪———————————

Table of Contents

Author BIO, Photo,
Amazon Page, Web-site,
Twitter, Blog, & Contact Information

Where Lightning Strikes

Learning the New Language

When I waited for light,
there came darkness.

Job 30: 26

First Day of German Class

We unearth the books in cartons behind his desk,
their pages crisp, their bindings unbroken. The boys

are the only ones brave enough to touch them. We
girls don't dare. While we admire the books, the German

sweeps in, wearing a black uniform with silver
buttons, gleaming medals, and a sunlight halo.

We scurry to our seats, whispering amazement
at his face. In the desk behind me, Anna leans

forward to breathe my very thoughts. When the German's
eyes caress her, she blushes, bows her head, doesn't

speak again. I imagine myself seventeen
and beautiful, my unruly hair less coarse, less

dark. I imagine his gazing at me the way my
brother Abram stares at the girls with pale braids who

pass our house each day on the walk home from school. The
German's ardent words enthrall us. While he talks, he

strokes his rugged palm with his baton, strolls between
the rows of desks. His boy assistants press in our

hands our first new word: black lettering on a gold,
six-pointed star. His voice glides, pirouettes, wreathes

'round us. *Soon,* we think, *we, too, will own these words.* When he
pauses beside my desk, I glance up. *Édesem,*

he whispers, trembling, and I know that he, too, has
been longing to play this part. My lovely fair hair

strays across my eyes and throat as he leans nearer;
then I feel the color of his eyes, and I taste

his sweet breath. Anna's fingers gouge my shoulder
as he strides to the front of the room, eclipsing

the light. The next moment, a train's roar turns him to
a mime, its acrid smoke stinging the autumn air.
✡

Landscape, With Figures

This is the night they came to take father: the year
the potatoes all blackened and swelled, the year the

milk-cow lay down in the coarse straw, never to get
up again, the year the winds broke all the windows,

and the baby crying, crying all the long night.
We children were at the table, clenching our spoons,

when they came for him. Papa said nothing, but he
shivered even in his heavy coat. Mama bit

her cracked knuckles, stared after him a long time from
the open door. Our soup cooled in its bowls. Later,

when the others had finally drifted to dreaming,
I crept downstairs to the kitchen. Mama rocked from

side to side, moaning, twisting and untwisting
a thin towel. I stood in the doorway, watching her,

the flickering firelight shadowing the hem
of my nightdress. *Natascha,* she said when she saw

me. Then she closed her eyes and raised her face to the
blank ceiling. I stood there, saying nothing. The wind

moaned. The fire hissed.
The night huddled in around us.
✡

Learning The New Language

He was capable of tossing off quite calmly,
between the soup and the vegetable course,
"I want to annihilate the Jews in Europe."

Albert Speer

It has repeatedly surprised me, in later
years, that scarcely any anti-Semitic remarks
of Hitler's have remained in my memory.

Albert Speer

With a formal bow, the manservant announces
dinner and, filled champagne glasses in hand, we laugh

ourselves into the dining hall. Margarete is
seated opposite me at table; she smiles and

shows me her crossed fingers: the rumor is there are
great things in store for me. I cross mine, smile back, then

greet my dinner companions. At long last, the one
we've been expecting enters, wearing a tie that

doesn't quite match his jacket. He goes to the head
of the table and sits down. Like children, we knock

our silver against the china, set the crystal
down too heavily, but he never scolds. Between

the soup and vegetable courses, he begins to
speak. I lean toward the sound, but the words elude me.

I ask the old man beside me to interpret:
he nods, mumbling something incoherent. Meanwhile,

Margarete chats with a uniformed man on her
left. My head spins from all the alcohol and the

efforts to decipher. I concentrate instead
on my salad, pushing the onions to the side,

chewing in silence. With a great scraping of chairs,
the others stand, lifting their champagne. Then someone

nudges my elbow, guiding my hand toward my own
filled glass: I raise mine as well. Margarete shows crossed

fingers again. We drink. The new words spark in my
glass: its stem is slender, cool, hard. Later that night,

at home, undressing for bed, Margarete chatters
in the brand new way, and my fingers tremble on

my shirt buttons. I go to the window. Outside,
the snowman the children built, turned to ice, lies on

his side. New snow covers his mouth and eyes. His scarf
flutters, trying to shake off the smothering and

glittering white. I whisper him one of the new
words. The glass against my forehead is smooth, cold, hard.
✡

When The Dancer Becomes The Dance

Art is not the truth. Art is the lie
that helps us understand the truth.

Pablo Picasso

The phonograph whirs as its needle lowers, then
violins whisper the key into the lock on

the door, his pistol from the holster. He lays it
on the desk. The flame wavers before lighting his

cigarette. Alone, he paces in the office,
fingers brushing gleaming wood of the furniture

as he passes. The dark ballerina appears,
begins dancing to his music. The violins

lift her into *arabesque penchée*. He reaches
out to stroke her cheek, but she shimmers into the

shaved scarecrow-girl, into dust flittering in the
sunlight cascading through closed windows. Winter light

embraces him before he dons his uniform
jacket. As each button sighs, he becomes the still

partner in the ballerina's *pas de deux,* his
hands skimming smooth fabric. The ballerina and

8

violins encircle him. Each time he tries to
take her hand, the other girl touches his, then blends

into sunlight, pure on his outstretched hand. Bass and
violas glide him to the chair behind his desk.

He readies the weapon, caresses the metal.
The ballerina pirouettes *en manège* as

he holds its steel length to his jaw, cheek, and temple,
eyeing her. With each whirl toward the windows, the light

flickers her into the pale girl, into itself.
Ballerina, scarecrow-girl, sunlight, violins

dance *ritardando*. When they glint into the pale girl
again, the trigger jerks under his finger.

✡

The late autumn sun croons to his back as he writes.
He rises, paces, smoking foreign cigarettes.

The paper mountains on his desk avalanche. He
flicks on music, pours a drink, resettles himself

behind the desk. Violins harmonize with the
scratching of his pen. He re-builds some paper hills,

signs others. Suddenly, from beyond his window:
shouting, swearing: *Schmutzige Jude. Hure.* He

twists toward the window, views his guard goading one of
the prisoners: a pale girl, a shaved scarecrow in

faded garb, seems to move, *lento,* to the music.
Toller Hure. the guard growls. The officer shouts

to the man to silence him. The violins soar,
buoy the girl in *arabesque.* Her motion fixes

him: his cigarette burns his fingers. He dashes it,
curses. He positions the phonograph nearer.

The frail scarecrow floats, turns. She pauses after the
crescendo, the neck of her gown fluttering, eyes

opaque. The guard escorts her with the butt of his
rifle. Every morning after, the Kommandant's

music swells his garden, the girl's stiff body sways
near his window, the sun glows on his ashen hair.

✡

Before the curtain falls on the first movement of
the new ballet, one of his friends has declared the

five of them desperately in love with the *prima
ballerina.* He scoffs, but through the second half,

the purity of her *grand jeté,* silver-white
in the darkened theatre, infatuates his

blue-green eyes. After the curtain call, he lets his friends
persuade him backstage. Her lashes are long on her

flushed cheeks. Not having brought roses, they present her
cigarettes. Her laugh forgives. He has smoked his, so

when they nudge him, his uniform pockets are bare.
He clicks his heels, bows formally: *My duty and*

obedience, leans to graze his lips on her cool
fingers. His friends hush. On their way home, they spy an

old couple with yellow stars. Their truncheons and boots
remind them that they are breaking summer curfew.

His brass knuckles order them to remember who
they are. Then he and his friends saunter home, humming

tunes from the ballet. He hymns the black of her eyes,
the street-lamps casting haloes around his blond hair.

✡

In the humming auditorium, the spectacled
speaker raises his arm, shouts: *We are the sword of*

the revolution, and, all around, blond boys leap,
cheering, to their feet. They worship the soldiers

guarding the speakers. He and his friends parade the
brilliance of their own black uniforms. *We pledge to*

you loyalty and bravery, they repeat, bass
and tenor expanding the auditorium.

We swear obedience, they chant, *even unto
death, as God is our witness.* Then they may salute.

He cheers *continuo.* Next, at their permanent
table in the local tavern, the age-mates toast

each other, serenade their guns, practice aiming.
That night, in his room, he and music salute the

mirror, admire the contour of the weapon.
He mimes his new face, directs the melody from

the phonograph with the gun, abruptly salutes.
The bleached curtains applaud, arching toward him. He grins,

hugs himself, dances to bed, collapses, pistol
swaying in violins' rhythm. *Meine Ehre heisst Treue,*

he refrains: *My honor is my loyalty.* The
spring breezes shroud his eyes, lullaby him to dreams.
✡

The Dead Bodies That Line The Streets

When you live close to the graveyard,
you can't weep for everybody.

Russian proverb

The dead understand all this,
and keep in touch.

Charles Wright

Dead:
Out of Play Though Not
Necessarily Out of the Game

Submit to the present evil,
lest a greater one befall you.

Phaedrus
Fables

My request for transfer is denied, this time with
an angry phone call from my superiors in

Berlin. *You'll stay where you are. Unless you want to
return to the front.* No, thank you. No, not even

for another Iron Cross. It's hard to see them
every day, but it's harder still to see friends fall.

So what can I do? What can any of us do?
Marta's letter has been on my desk a week. She'll

worry if I don't write soon, but I don't have the
courage to answer it. Besides, what is there to

say to her? One of the inmates slipped yesterday
in the muck and mire of the camp's yard, and three others

rushed over to pick him up. I could have lifted him
with only one hand, he was so thin and frail. A mere

scarecrow. When they saw me watching them, their eyes, just
for one brief moment, turned less opaque. No one moved.

But I felt almost as if I should do something,
say something, anything, to make them understand.

Then their eyes clouded again. Like always. They clutched
their fallen comrade and dragged themselves away from

me, leaving me standing there, the baton cold and
hard in my hand, the snow falling all around us.
✡

The Dead Bodies That Line The Streets

chatter and snipe at me constantly, as if I
were responsible for their being there. But I

ignore all their remonstrative and sarcastic
remarks. Favoritism or fraternization

with the enemies of the State is forbidden,
and I won't tarnish my reputation or my

family name by giving them special privileges
that might alleviate their misery. Don't they

deserve what's happening to them? Didn't they kill
our Lord and Savoiur? My best friend Kurt, though he wears

the same uniform as I, is not as cautious,
not as circumspect. *Why shouldn't we be paid to*

do our job in this God-forsaken Ghetto and
be rewarded for sometimes not doing it as

well? he says before he slips behind the bricked wall
or behind the stack of bodies with his latest

protectee, a beautiful girl who hardly looks
Jewish at all. *We're much closer to the Front than*

we are to home, he reminds me, buttoning his
uniform after he returns. *Such things are routine*

at the Front, he says, and he should know since
his brother was killed there only last spring. Sometimes,

I admit, I'm tempted when I see some lovely
girl who'd do anything for only a bit of

brown bread or a piece of sausage. I even caught
myself wondering what one of them might do for

a bite of chocolate or some cigarettes. But they
heard my innocent musings and have fastened their

rolled-back eyes on me ever since. I get angry,
threaten them, poke them with my bayonet: *leave me*

be, I shout. But their gaping mouths *tsk tsk tsk* at
me until I light up a cigarette and toss

the still-burning match onto one of their lolling
tongues. That usually silences them. These bodies

should be carted away and dumped somewhere, but Kurt
claims they're here as a symbol to the living. As

far as I can determine, these beggars ignore
their dead. Instead they scurry around, stealing food

from each other, trying to bribe me or one of
the other fellows, hurling themselves over the

wall or through the wire. And the dead bodies that line
the streets certainly don't care about their living

comrades, or they wouldn't lie around spying and
gossiping to annoy me, trying to prevent

me from doing my job. The bodies that line the
streets should be hauled away and incinerated,

their ashes scattered to the heavens. Then I could
perform my duties without interference, eat

meals without tasting dust,
sleep at night without dreams.
✡

Alexandria Constantinova Szeman

Cutthroat:
A Player Who Plays For Himself

(Auschwitz 1944)

No one is capable of understanding you who
is not capable of doing the same...himself.

Pablo Picasso

✡

In cramped and humid cattle-cars, gold stars glimmer
on coats, shirts, dresses, while shadowed heads drift and sway

in the tracks' rhythm. Children fall asleep and dream
about thick winter soup, studded with turnips and

potatoes. A boy bumps into the waste-bucket,
overturning it, and dozens of hands cover

raw noses, muffling the curses. In a corner
a girl leans her head against the boards. At last the

train screeches to a halt, then wood scrapes on wood as
the doors open. *Los, Los, Aussteigen,* the voices

shout as people tumble out into the darkness.
One of the uniforms barks at her bluer eyes.

Where Lightning Strikes

✡

No. It's a dream. I only dream that the German
officer comes over to the line of women

standing motionless against a bloodied wall, his
boots gleaming in the red clay, his baton butting

cold and hard against my jaw, his eyes on me, his
Sie sind alle Huren, the mud's choking sounds as

he strides away, stepping over all the bodies.
Yes, a dream. It must be a dream I feel nothing.

✡

I lie. It's no dream. It is not even a nightmare.
But I've learned how to escape. When they go to the

showers scream *This one's my brother* or *That one's my
child.* Run up to embrace them. The soldiers will point

their guns. Pretend you don't see them. Weep. Beg. Cover
their hands with your desperate kisses. They'll snarl, *Toller*

Jude. Pretend that you are. March. Salute. Then grab
anything close to you wearing swastika.

✡

One girl finds a way out. The German officer
keeps her in his special place, gives her cognac

and champagne and caviare. She says nothing when he
slides over her. He doesn't mind her silence, her

stillness. Afterward, he falls asleep, and she walks
anywhere she pleases, even out among the

rest of them. They won't speak to her. Some spit. Soldiers
call out to her but she only knows German in

dreams. She used to dream of grassy fields, towering
sunflowers, Jan's callused hands and soft lips. Now she

dreams dark bread, potatoes, bits of greasy butter,
his face, his hands, his mouth, his panting sweating weight.

✡

I lie. It's not that difficult. And it's not that
painful. Besides, any time it could end. Just choose

a day to caress the woven steel fence. That will
do it. Or when the guards in the towers call to

you, don't turn around. Or perhaps they'll say nothing,
but you'll feel the freedom they give you. Or the dogs

will run to greet you, their mouths open wide. The way
doesn't matter. No nightmare's worse than our waking.
✡

Lager-Lieder

(Camp Songs)

Not last night but the night before, twenty-
four Gestapo came knocking at the door.

As we ran out, they ran in, and this is
what they shouted then: Oh, *Ju-den, Ju-den,*

turn around. Oh, *Ju-den, Ju-den,* touch the
ground. *Ju-den, Ju-den,* get out of town.

Fly away, fly away, fly away home.
Your house is on fire, your children alone.

Black currant, red currant, raspberry tart,
this is the day and hour you'll depart.

All you *Juden*, how you wander, from one
land in-to another. *Führer* promised

Aryan fear — We'll have no more *Juden*
here. All these homeless *Juden,* lo, where shall

these poor *Juden* go? Send them east. No, send
them west. No, send them where they're loved the best.

One suitcase, two parcel, three rucksack, four,
five suitcase, six parcel, seven rucksack,

more — *Füh-rer* said to spare the Ger-mans and
these are too Jew. You, left. You, right.

23

First Jew I see tonight. I wish I may,
I wish I might, kill the Jews I see tonight.

Pretty, pretty Irma, striding through the
campgrounds. Shining boots and bright whip, flying

through the campgrounds. Smile, Irma, smile. Flash your
big blue eyes. Shoot to the east, and shoot to

the west, then shoot the Jew that you love best.
Kommandant, Kommandant, *Führer's* man, bake

me a Jew as fast as you can. Strip him
and beat him and mark him with *J*. Put him

in the oven for a *Judenrein* day.
Red cherries, blue berries, blackberry jam,

look to the chimneys — you'll see where I am.
Mama, Mama, I am sick. Send for the

doctor, quick, quick, quick. Doctor comes and says,
Too bad: this one's surely meant for gas. Nurse

then comes and sighs, *Too bad: Mama also
will not pass.* Papa, Papa, here we die;

you will find us in the sky. When the smoke
has cleared away, it will be a sunny

day. Ring around the roses, we're the sons
of Moses. Ashes. Ashes. Jews fall down.

Now we lay us down to sleep; we pray the
Lord our souls to keep. If we die before

we wake, we pray the
Lord our souls to take.
✡

On The Other Hand,

death: not everyone's favorite topic
of conversation, I know, but some things

they have to be talked about, they can't be
avoided, you'll get used to it. We get

used to anything. Look at me: as stout
as good *challah* I used to be, and now:

matzoh. Open the door from this side. But
what a man I was. What arms I had. The

envy of men, desire of girls for
miles. What shoulders I had. From hoisting those

sacks of flour. Stir them around. Don't look:
just stir. And muscles from kneading. Did I

knead. Day in, day out. In the beginning,
lying down on my pillow at night hurt,

my shoulders were so sore. I learned; you will,
too. But more bread than anyone I made,

better, cheaper. From miles they came to buy
my breads. And my ovens weren't even so

large as these: I could afford such ovens?
Only toward the end did the fires burn

all night, so no crumbling bricks in mine. Here,
take them out this way. Now the fires will

not go out. The beasts have been sent among
us. They rob us of our children, destroy

our cattle. Cattle they never touched, let
alone destroyed. Drag this to the door: scrape

the ashes into it. Cattle — grazing,
sleeping, as if it were *Shabbas.* We take

the fat and burn it in the ovens: it
goes faster that way. One set of clothes we

take off, another we put on, and to
another place we carry the ashes.

Don't worry. This is your first day: you'll soon
forget to notice. That which remaineth

of the flesh and of the bread shall we burn
with the fire. Only better to eat the

bread, they would mind? Worse than yours my first day
was. For months I don't see my in-laws I'm

working so hard. My wife is complaining —
all these strangers and you're never at home —

she's worried. My first day here, who do I
see? My wife and her parents. What do I

do? Kiss them? Cry tears of reunion? Of course
not: foolish I've never been. Here, work is

all we know: people we don't recognize.
It is written: ten women shall bake in

one oven — even if they're *mussulmans,*
into one oven, don't put that many.

Otherwise, another catastrophe
like a few months ago: new helpers we

have, but does anyone teach them? Fans they
don't turn on. Ovens they overheat. Then,

Pow. The wall explodes. Three days we don't work.
We don't work, we don't eat. We don't eat, we

bake. After, among ourselves, we agree:
Never again. From now on, we teach the

right way. Us they will not swallow up in
their wrath. Us the fire shall not devour.

Us the land of our enemies shall not
eat up. Our ashes they shall not scatter

into the wind, God willing. We are few
in number. And on the other hand, death.
✡

White-on-White

Nothing is as beautiful
as two varieties of the
same color side by side.

Edgar Degas

✡

With a dull rattle, his office door unlocks and
she stands up in the shadows, her bare head veiled by

moonlight. He stumbles to the chair, without lights,
his boots and his labored breathing the only language

between them. Smoke from his Italian cigarettes
drifts toward the ceiling. With one hand he unbuckles

his holster and service dagger, clanks them onto
the wooden desktop, then undoes his uniform

buttons. She smokes, watching him, till he kneels before
her, his bared left arm across her lap. A scar in

the shape of her six-pointed star calls to her. Like
a *prima ballerina,* she unfolds one leg,

taps pointed toes against his chest. Then, clumsy and
inexperienced, he falters. For his *faux pas,*

her heel on his collarbone demotes him to
a role in the *corps*. Clutching his dangling arm, he weeps.

✡

In the middle of the night, she slips into bed.
Beneath the blankets, her thigh brushes his as the

flat of the blade of his service dagger caresses his
cheek. The prick awakes him, and he bounds aside just

as the glittering knife thrusts into his pillow.
He crouches in the corner, his chest heaving, his

hair disheveled, as she solemnly carves up the
bedclothes. Her vague song scrapes the ice from the windows.

✡

He sloughs off the dampened wool of his uniform,
kicks aside his boots, ties her wrists to the bedposts

before he wakes her. Smoke from his French cigarettes
and the chimneys perfume him. When he thrusts deep and

hard into her, her teeth on his shoulder draw blood.
On the far side of the room, his weapons shudder.

✡

She kneels, pries the drink from his hand, and rolls up his
left sleeve. With his black pen she draws her six-pointed

star on his forearm. He snorts with laughter, saying,
Jetzt bin ich ein Jude, but she shakes her head, drags

his wrist, traps it between her ribs and arm. With bent
head, she cuts her six-pointed name into his arm.

With his service dagger. She sighs, raises her face.
Jetzt bist du mein Jude. He gazes up at her.

The phonograph needle stammers at record's end.
Her bright eyes swallow light from the camp around them.
✡

Sofie and Anna

(for Anna Brunn Ornstein,
who survived Auschwitz)

I did not write to console you.

✡

For years, cowbells wakened Anna, coaxed her to her
parents' bed where their breathing lulled her to dreamless

dozing until the late morning sun and breakfast
duties beckoned. One morning, a strange hush wakens

Anna instead. Heart pounding, Anna searches the
house, discovers Sofie on the back porch, carding

wool. *Mama,* she sighs, kneeling beside her, laying
her head in her lap, but Sofie doesn't hear her,

sees only the dark mountains huddled on the far
horizon. Back in her own bed, layers of wool

blanket over Anna's head muffle her sobs and
block out the keening cry of a frightening wind.

✡

Everything must fit exactly in the rucksack:
heavy boots, wool coat, sweater, cap, crust of brown bread.

31

After Sofie finishes, she empties it all,
begins again, *ritardando.* Her son struggles

into the last layer of heavy wool clothing,
into the leather straps of the bulging rucksack.

Anna abandons the laundry she's been folding
and comes over to them. But Sofie shrugs off her

embrace, stands in the open doorway, concentrates
on the rucksack until her belovèd son, her

favorite child, disappears beyond the distant trees.
The rose stone tiles are cool under Anna's bare feet.

✡

Bayonets, pistols, and nail-boots shepherd Sofie
and Anna to the train-station where cattle-cars

swallow all those with bundles on their backs, then yank
away, clanking rhythmically beyond the haze

of summer landscapes. Inside the overcrowded,
locked cars, the dulled frightened weeping eyes, the stench, and

the women crying out in labor are pummeled
into one heap. Then a hoarse chant stirs them: *Rain. Rain.*

Desperate hands scratch away clutching hands to thrust through
the steel grating with tiny metal cups. Anna

breathes in the pale glimmer of Sofie's six-pointed
gold. Throughout the darkest night, the train gambols on.

✡

When they step out of the train, blue fog fondles them.
In the camp, uniforms shout *Los, los. Aussteigen,*

aussteigen. An officer with a horsewhip sends
Papa one way, Sofie and Anna another.

A white-bloused, navy-skirted orchestra of young
girls plays sprightly tunes as fence-signs chant *Arbeit macht*

frei. The chimneys applaud as printed inscriptions
on picture postcards that are addressed to distant

relatives sing the latest song: *from Waldsee — we
are doing very well here. We have work and we*

are well treated. We await your arrival, and,
beneath the printed words, she is forced to write, *love, Sofie.*

✡

After dawn-whistles shrill them awake — *Zählappel* —
the grey columns of tattered clothes sway in march-time,

gather together in the camp's yard, then wait. Wait.
The Kommandant arrives, counts them off so he and

his pistol can kiss them. *Eins. Zwei. Drei. Kuss.* Holding
Anna's hand tightly, Sofie trades places with her

daughter to become the *kiss.* But the Death's-Header
gets bored, yawns, and canters away. In amazement,

Anna touches her mother's arm, but Sofie's gaze
never leaves the Kommandant's galloping white horse.

✡

One night, a bare bulb over the kitchen door shines
on the camp cook and her girlfriend as they sponge each

other's flat breasts. Anna pleads for the dingy, grey
water, carries it to her mother. Sofie clings to Anna's neck,

wakes up, then pulls away. The filthy water cools
the sores on Sofie's cracked skin. When Anna is ill

in the camp's hospital, Sofie finds an apple
core in the road, retrieves it, saves it to offer,

a week later, as a gift for Anna's birthday.
Anna eats. The window is cold on Sofie's cheek.

✡

One day, the sun and silence awaken Anna.
The others still sleep. Beyond the window, the gates

are open and the camp is deserted. All the
sentries' towers are completely empty. After

the Kommandant's insignia were torn from his
jacket, he fled into the surrounding forest.

Anna wakes the others. The women wait. Later,
a Russian on a motorcycle, dust-covered

and giddy with liberation, invites all the
women to a party. They stare at each other.

The teeming pantries are emptied of the cognac,
champagne, and caviare. A few inmates with shears

entertain two female uniforms. All over
the camp, fires burn. Anna finds her mother, a

blanket trailing from her thin shoulders. She holds out
her hand. *Annushka,* she says. Anna sobs. Sofie

dances her daughter into her arms, and, while winds
around them keen, coos her the ancient lullaby.
✡

Survivor: One Who Survives

After the first death,
there is no other.

Dylan Thomas

Bone-on-Bone

Your blood be upon your
own heads; I am clean.

Acts 18:6

Yes, I heard. They told me at a dinner party.
They wept as they shook their heads, pale moths fluttering

around your extinguished flame, while I drank myself
sick in the corner. We would have protected you

from interrogation, punishment, betrayal.
There I stood, surrounded by your orphans, shoulders

hunched, eyes wide, like lonely-eyed deer in a snowdrift,
awaiting some unmistakable sign, some hope,

some reassurance, some *No, it was not in vain.*
All these years, with nothing to be forgiven but

our falling asleep in dark confessionals, or
spending whole summers without praying, or stealing

a few innocent kisses from the village girls.
We were like dancing fawns, skirting their world, but you

were always the braver one. Now, I'm confused. I
have something, I'm sure. I can't sleep. My wife says I

just waste time. But I was thinking of you again
tonight. How could you, of all people? What was it

that made you bite down on the silvery capsule,
leaving us with the bitter taste in our mouths? Why

didn't you take us with you? When the moon slipped from
behind the dark clouds, it reminded me that soon

your eyes might meet mine again, like they did that long
ago night over the stilled body. Both of us

hid then. Now I'm the only one left. My wife calls
to me, *Come away from the window on such a*

dark night; it isn't safe, Albert. It isn't right.
I don't listen. I don't want to. Sometimes I think

I want the pain of bone-on-bone — unbearably
fierce. And as strong — almost — as things I used to feel.
✡

Survivor: One Who Survives

The only difference between a madman
and myself is that I am not mad.

Salvador Dali

Four or five times a day, steamy baths fog away
her past until the skin puckers, then heavy towels
unburden her. She frees her hair, shakes it until

it caresses her back and thighs: she has not cut
it since liberation, will not allow scissors
in the house. Her husband doesn't complain any

longer. Early each morning, she stretches clean starched
sheets tautly over the sturdy mattress, then crawls
between them when trains clank the tracks half a mile from

the house. She still insists on accompanying
the children to school, only lately has she
allowed them to return on their own. They keep their

backpacks in their lockers, remind each other to
discard their apple cores before arriving home
so she can't retrieve them and hide them under her

pillow. She wears long sleeves even in summer. The
children invent elaborate stories about the
blue-black numbers scratched on her left forearm. She still

flinches at the hint of a uniform, and still
imagines an extra point on the gold star on
the village Christmas tree, stares until her husband

liberates her. The children don't bring any of
their friends home. She goes to bed early each night, and
her husband guards her anxious dozing, smoothing hair

from her face. In the darkness, those voices shout *zu
Fünf* while a train without brakes plunges into deep
tunnels winding ever deeper into the earth.
✡

Unframed Daguerreotype

This early method of taking pictures on plates
of silver or silvered copper, this method of

making pictures which is not engraving because
the image to be retained is not gouged into

stone glass wood, this forming of faces on plates of
silver may have captured once a portrait of my

lover. Some plate of silvered copper buried in
lost archives, a scratched and abandoned artist's plate

may show the contours of my lover's face, but the
only photograph of him in my possession

is etched on my body. Scars on my left calf from
my descent that long ago night, my stepping down

from the body-heat of the train to the blinding
bright of the platform frieze, from the cramped crowd of the

hissing train to the spotlighted and luggage-strewn
platform, hesitating as I went, stumbling in

his darkened path, I heard his dog's throaty whisper
pierce the noise and the bustle at the instant I

felt his teeth tattoo the calf of my wayward leg.
The photograph of my lover is sketched in the

knit of bone from my first deceit, the bone-woven
defiance told not in lover-binding dark but

in the light, the lie revealed not in shadows with
shame-bent head but in the brilliant afternoon, the

defiant act exposed not with shuddering in
the glare of his position but with a sneer that

a simple girl and his captive lover besides
had helped three others escape his domain, that I

a conquered girl had aided three whom he despised
elude his black-gloved grasp, that I, a girl, and a

rather plain one at that, with raised grin revealed to
the baton of his anger the escape of three

through his fence-designated boundaries, that a
girl dare flaunt the freeing of three with bread-stuffed and

coin-lined pockets through his steel net, three through the wire
laden with foods and monies secreted from his

fenced and guarded larder while he slept in the bed
I had abandoned, deserted in sleep by a

pale girl with shaved head whose flouted success earned the
crack and snap of collarbone and ribs. My lover's

face is there in the palm scars from the *snick snick snick*
of the match till the flame caught, illuminated

his face bent over the flicker of palm-cupped light,
his blue eyes sleep-dulled over the flickering, his

full lips pouting into a smile around the French
cigarette, behind the cigarette's glow his lips

full and rose and smiling behind the wisps of grey
smoke, his smiling above the flame pressed hard into

my open palm, his eyes over the flare of thin
matchwood buried in the hand opened to stroke the

wind-burnt cheek, the palm lifted to caress the gaunt
cheek, re-carved so that no one, not even I, would

recognize him, the lean cheek re-formed now so that
not even the frail girl with six-pointed gold, if

she were to collide one day with his dark-coated
woolen-scarfed form rounding the corner less than half

a block from her apartment, even she would not
remember the curve of the cheek, the line of the

nose, re-made so not even the frail girl and I,
bundled against the drift of winter winds, if we

were, with bent head, to turn the corner, crash into
this stranger scowling through snow-clouds, even we should

not be able to connect his newborn face to
that which he once called himself. But here on our left

forearm blue-black on the curve of my left forearm
are scraped the numbers of his old name: *scratch scratch scratch*.
✡

In Pursuit Of Our Own Shadows

The first time I met her, she wasn't at all like
the townspeople had been saying. Not cold, aloof,

haughty as everyone claimed because she didn't
join in Saturday sewing bees, or invite folks

in for lemonade in the late afternoons, or
attend Sunday morning church services. But I

knew she couldn't be like folks said. I just had to
meet her, talk to her, so I picked out my best short

story as a present, the one about the girl
who turns invisible, which makes her four brothers

sad forever after. I printed it on the
flowered paper from the General Store, then tied

it with my pink hair ribbon. Saturday, after
chores, I threaded white ribbons through my two braids, held

my story gingerly so it wouldn't wrinkle
or get crushed, and practiced my words on the way to

her house. More than I wished I were a grownup, I
wanted to be a writer. Not the kind who wrote

newspaper stories or birthday rhymes, but one whose
books were in libraries. She was a writer. My

hands were sweaty-cold when I knocked on the wood of
the screen-door. I wiped them on the front of my dress.

When she answered, I lifted the ribboned story
with *Welcome* because that's how Mama and Daddy

greeted company. She stared at me through the screen
without a sound. Just when my arm was starting to

feel shaky and weak, the door creaked hesitantly
open. The papers' unrolling were the only

words between us. She lowered the story, with a
look in her eyes that stilled me, then placed her palm on

my head. That was how I met Azelia. Even
her name was an exotic flower that never

bloomed here. Her words, whose accent caused complaints, glittered
so that I wanted to sparkle them for others.

Her curly short hair that Grandma called *Shocking* was
grander than anyone's, even from picture shows:

I prayed I could cut mine like that. And I didn't
care about the blue-black numbers scratched on her left

forearm. While she re-read my story, I ate some
sugar cookies and sipped lemonade. Then she said

it was the best present anyone had given
her would I please do her the honor of paying

a visit next Saturday. My feet skipped, danced home.
She lived, wrote, typed in that crumbling house, and she was

never cold or unkind or haughty. She wasn't
like anyone claimed. Until the day he arrived.

I saw him first because Azelia was in the
Kitchen, and I was on the porch swing. He stayed in

his car so long I thought he must have the wrong house.
Then the car door jerked open. There he stood: so tall

and fierce blond that he looked sun-branded. I rose as
he and his white-blond hair and dark boots mounted the

porch steps. Azelia was already at the door,
holding a tray with ice-filled glasses. He nodded

but didn't venture beyond the porch edge. Through the
screen's grey, I glimpsed the white of her knuckles gripping

the tray. His right hand clenched one of her books, and her
face was as it had been when she caught me in her

library, glancing through it: *The Dead Bodies That
Line* . . . but the slim volume of poems was ripped from my

hands before I'd heard her enter. She swayed, shaking,
the book clutched to her breast, saying *No, this wasn't*

meant for you. The glasses shuddered and clinked against
each other. *Minna,* she said, *come back tomorrow.*

That night, I didn't want to eat dinner. Mama
checked my forehead to see if I were ill. When I

told about him, they fluttered around, insisting
he was a suitor. I changed into my nightdress,

shivered under the thin blanket. By next morning,
the preacher's wife knew his name, and under the shade

of summer green, how the church ladies buzzed. My feet
dragged on the walk to her house. My hair ribbons trailed

vague patterns in the road dust. His car was parked by
the side of the house. I crept nearer, peeked over

the edge of the open library window. There,
amongst the silenced books, his voice echoed, dark and

guttural. As he spoke, he leaned slightly toward her,
his hair ashen, his open-palmed hands entreating.

Azelia paced haltingly before him, shaking
her head, muttering words as strange as his. A fierce

cry from her arrested his voice. Under her cries,
his head bowed. After the sobbing had swallowed her

protests, his insistent, incomprehensible
words flowed again. As she strode past, he reached out, brushed

her arm. Azelia lashed free of him, hands flailing,
her cry ripping the tense air between them. Tears

splotched the front of my dress as I rushed home, his words
and her cries tripping my hurrying feet. For weeks

after, I invented excuses to avoid
visiting, escaped to bed early each night, lay

in the darkness, listening to night sounds. Then one
Sunday, before church services, her voice, asking

after me, floated up from the living room. I
raced to the top of the stairs, nightgown fluttering.

Despite Mama's frown and Grandma's protestations,
Azelia managed to wrest permission for me

to spend the last week before school at her house. I
washed, dressed, and packed before Daddy had poured her a

second cup of tea. She carried my bag. *I've missed
you, Minna.* I kicked at some roadside plants, then made

my shoulders wide with a huge breath: *What does this Klaus
want?* Azelia's step faltered. She halted, turned, her

face pale. *How did you know his name?* I shrugged, bent to
pluck some blushing clover. *Everyone knows.* I wound,

rewound, the frail stem about my fingers. She sighed.
Our breathing and footsteps preoccupied us the

day's remainder. That night, in the unfamiliar
bed, just drifting into haziness, I bolted

as her scream pierced me. Her bedclothes and her nightgown
glowed white in the moon's dusty light. I offered to

stay in case she dreamt again. She folded back the
covers and I crawled in beside her. *Were you lost?*

Her arms tugged me close. *No, but I was somewhere far
from here,* she admitted, stroking my hair. *The place*

that put those numbers on your arm? Her choked, faint *Yes*
wound my thin arms into a promise hugging her

close, tight, so she could feel my heartbeat, so she would
remember, even in sleep, that she was here. She

pressed her damp cheek to my forehead, and we drifted
to anxious dozing. On our last night, we made bread,

to thank Mama and Daddy for allowing the
visit. My fingers traced designs on the floured

table while Azelia kneaded the bulky dough.
What does Klaus want? Her hands stopped, embedded in the

sticky dough. I memorized the blue of her eyes.
I don't know, Minna. I stroked the butter into

one of the iron pans. *Does he love you?* Her breathing
was woven with the rhythmic bread thuds. I finished

one pan, shoved it aside, started another. *Do
you love him?* Her hands brusquely chased hair from her eyes

and forehead. Wiping her hands on her apron, she
left the kitchen, returned, bearing one of her books.

She offered the slim volume until my fingers
trembled around it. The dull slap of dough shook the

table. I swallowed, glanced down. *The Dead Bodies That
Line The Streets.* On Azelia's inner left forearm,

blue-black scratches peeped out from beneath her rolled-up
sleeve. I found the first poem, began to read. Outside,

in lengthening shadows, a male songbird crooned his
plaintive hymn, melancholy-sweet as the lowing

of a lone night train. But his mate would not answer.
Azelia's face mirrored the white of the bread. Her

book's words haunted me, like some dream-songs I'd murmured
in childhood, but forgotten, or lost, on waking.
✡

Alexandria Constantinova Szeman

Those Who Claim We Hated Them

and resented their return from the war,
lie. Why, we wept at their restoration

almost as if they were our own fallen
comrades, who lay buried in lands with strange,

unpronounceable names. We crowded our
doors and windows as their homecoming

parades hobbled through our narrow village
streets, and we remarked to one another

how their shaved heads reminded us of the
years without meat, sugar, butter, coffee,

peace. But they lie who claim we despised them.
We didn't blame them because the drinking

water from nearby streams had been choked by
ashes. They weren't responsible for the

years that our clothes and hair were infested
by the chimneys' stench when the wind drifted

toward our town. How could we resent them, the
children least of all, even if they did

knock on our doors and tug on the knobs when
we most craved solitude: just as Sunday's

chicken with apples and onions was placed,
steaming, on the table, or just after

the quilts had warmed our entwined and drowsy
bodies. Hate them? No, we pitied the frail

waifs, who pleaded entrance merely because
our houses and land had once belonged to

their fathers and mothers, who *tap tap tapped*
at the glass just because the light glowed through the

windowpane, who stared at us, dumbfounded,
though we had settled here years since, and had

long ago disposed of the abandoned
clothing, the framed photographs, the faded

curtains and furnishings. Nevertheless,
we apologized. Our wives patted their

shaved heads, and pressed into their outstretched hands
the cold remains of Friday's potato

pancakes. We clicked our tongues in sympathy
at the blue-black scratchings on their forearms.

But we had all suffered during the war.
We suffered, as they did. We had only

feigned gaiety at their misfortunes, to
convince our oppressors to spare our homes.

We only pretended fidelity,
to save our brothers, our cousins, our sons.

We cheered and applauded the great chimneys'
belching only to protect our wives, our

daughters, ourselves. They lie who say our hate
caused their grief, who say we resented their

homecoming, who say that we despised their
resurrection in our new and ordered lives.
✡

Letter to Sylvia

I praised the dead,
which are already dead,
more than the living,
who are yet alive.

Ecclesiastes 4:2

For years, whenever I thought of visiting you, a certain
music distracted me: I didn't know its final movement.
Last week, from the conservatory, that very tune beckoned:

I pleaded entrance until a girl with long fingers handed
me Beethoven's *Sonata quasi una Fantasia.*
I have spent the morning fumbling with it. My husband questions

reinforcing my melancholia, but as we have been
squalling, I ignore him, stutter over this language I love
but cannot read. He takes children, picnic, swimsuits to the lake

by the far meadow. I switch on Mozart's horn *concerti,* pour
a glass of scotch, wander our barn-house the fifteen minutes till
noon before allowing myself a sip. This makes me safe. For

days the youngest has refused baths, having heard me read aloud
a German recipe for soap, has been whining about a
woman with a broad patch of scar on her cheek roaming the hall

upstairs, silk cord dangling from her neck like a yellow cat's tail,
about the sweet of amethyst gas seeping through the floors of
his room at night. Since our stove is electric, his father has

forbidden his sipping any more wine with dinner. When the
children unearth a Ouija board in the cellar that only
spells *S-y-l-v-i-a,* I begin to understand: the

Nacht und Nebel around you has been ripped. I bury the board,
along with your picture. You know the bottom — I have yet to
open my eyes underwater, claiming family and writing

obligations. *Suicide is, after all, the opposite*
of a poem, Sexton preached, then rowed in nagging rain until her
arms were too limp to drag her back. The *Sonderkommando,* who

were to pluck her out with their nooses and hooks, gaped. She should have
known better than to trust your claim that you would rise nine times out
of the ash: even the Death's-Headers didn't recognize themselves

in the clinker, ground to fine dust and sifted into the stream.
The *Judengesetz* did not affect you, yet that last time you
tried to shed your skin, your safe-conduct didn't separate you

from others made stateless. Neither did Eichmann's *I can't shed my*
skin save him. Suddenly I have lost my children's faces. I
stumble through grass to where they splash and squeal in the lake's calm. *What*

is so real as the cry of a child? The screams that Höss timed: *three*
to fifteen minutes depending on climatic conditions.
Nightly, their cries seek me out: sharks' teeth sunk into my flesh, then

retracted, waiting for the blood loss to weaken me. I snap
off one or two, but row after row of razored pearl clamors
beneath the swollen gun, anxious to tattoo. Frau Ilse would

covet this specimen. Arielle explodes from the lake, hounds
one of her brothers to the fluttering blanket where I read.
These children are after something, with hooks and cries. She leans, drips

on your book, damps my cheek. Her brother's curls cool my bare thigh. He
sings one of his new hymns. Where were Frieda and Nicholas when
you entered your *Kazett?* Did you want to crush them back into

your body as petals of a rose fold in at night? Was your
greatest fear as Magda's: that at the last moment you would be
too weak? There is no mercy in the dark. Unpeeling its gauze

layers does not mean truth. I see you, coiled teratism, on
the kitchen floor, lips and cheeks poppies against parchment skin. I
yank Arielle close, call my other son in from dark waves, scrub

the wine that stains my pale skin, inhale my children's breathing, kiss
them. Even with six-pointed gold, hallucinations cannot
be controlled forever. Red on white doesn't always mean love.
✡

At The Point Where Lightning Strikes

nothing ever grows again. We knew this
even as children trailing Grandfather

after the storms to the woods beyond the
far field. His hair glowed white among the green

shadows, and his blue-veined hands caressed the
gutted carcass of the bolt-split tree. At

times only a limb would be severed, and
Grandfather's patience and the seasons' balm

would cauterize the wound. Sometimes the bolt
missed even the limb. On the ground beneath,

at the precise point of strike, the soil would
be petrified. Afterward, no tendrils

could penetrate the dull dead glaze of earth,
and the tree beside it was forever

reminded of its near encounter with
heat and fire and light. When we were young, we

heard all the stories about lightning: that
it never struck the same spot twice, that no

human being could survive a direct
hit, that God touched the earth with this fierce and

blinding light. As children, we believed them
all. When their first jagged bolt of fire ripped

father's job away and left six-pointed gold
scars on all the men's chests, Grandfather sewed

his war decorations all round. When he
went down into the streets, some of the old

neighbors congratulated him. A blond
stranger got off his bicycle to shake

his hand. Their next bolt separated us
from our school friends and branded our own breasts.

Mother sang while she stitched the scar to my
coat pocket. *How lucky you are, my son.*

Do you know how few may wear this star? My
feet skipped through the storm-littered streets until

I discovered the boys who had not been
struck. Their boots and fists and curses taught me

one of the very first lessons — lightning
burns. Neither Grandfather nor my parents

survived their next strike. They were too frail to
bear the ferocity of the light. I looked

at my feet and kept walking. Youth and the
years' balm cauterized the wounds, though nothing

grew in the seared spots. Still, none discovered
the scar hidden beneath my wilderness.

None traced the ragged outlines of this burnt
and petrified soil. In middle age, I

learned few new truths about lightning, except
that its graves should not be excavated.

Today, at the university, the
lightning struck again. I had just dismissed

my class and was hurrying to my next
lecture when a voice brushed me like the wind.

I turned. When her long fingers offered the
late essay, my reading glasses fell. In

the rush of fingers, papers, knees bumping,
slender legs covered by a sheer skirt, her

pale hair sweeping over the black tattoo
on my inner left forearm, her blue eyes

gazed up at me. *Jude,* she said. *Jude.*
For a moment, all was darkness. Silence.

Except for the hint of a tremor in
the scalded earth, at the exact point of

strike, and the startled breath of one flattened
by a blinding bolt from a darkened sky.
✡

The Day The Snakes Came

Wouldst thou have a
serpent sting thee twice?

William Shakespeare
The Merchant of Venice 4.1.69

We thought, at first, that we were imagining them:
that sliver of disturbed dust by the sidewalk, that

hint of damp on the kitchen floor. Then we thought they
were an aberration: the one found coiled in young

Markowitz's bathroom sink, the other around
the apple strudel in Mrs. Polski's icebox.

The beasts have been sent among us, said Leopold,
to rob us of our children and to destroy our

cattle. Since we knew he drank his meals, we shook our
heads, and pitied his daughter Leah who came each

night to drag her father home, his arms waving like
snakes. Then others began to talk. Everywhere, there

was snake talk: *It's been pretty dry the last few years;*
they're just looking for water. Old Farmer Johnson

must have turned up a lot of rocks in his field this
spring. If you don't bother them, they won't bother you.

Some people even laughed. Then our neighbors began
slicking back their hair. Our children practiced flicking

their tongues in front of the bathroom mirrors, and changed
their names to snake names. By September the snakes were

everywhere. Glistening black bodies swarmed over
the sidewalks, bubbled out of the water pipes, milled

out of morning cereal. Some tried to ignore
the snakes. They were the first to disappear. Others

argued: *They don't have any reason to hurt us.*
What have we done to them? If we don't bother them,

they won't bother us. They were next to vanish. A
few brave ones tried to learn snake words, to untangle

the slithering black unrest. Their facility
at languages could not save them. But most of us

tried to protect ourselves. The snakes caught us any
time: when we were gathering fruit in the garden,

when we reached into the basket of knitting, when
we crawled into bed at night. Then suddenly, one

spring day, the snakes were gone. A cold wind blew in their
place. We lost most of our village to the snakes. We

heard the same from neighboring towns. The wind chilled us.
We swept the brittle carcasses out of our homes,

replanted our gardens, and tried to rebuild new,
snake-less lives. The years passed. The wind blew cold, hard words

at us: *There must have been something to upset the*
snakes: they only attack to protect themselves. It

60

could never happen here. I never saw a snake
in my life. If they were here, they weren't in my house.

But we have taught our children about the snakes. We
teach them how to wield bats, how to ignore wispy

whispered snake charms, how to crush a snake's head with their
heels. Because late at night we hear them, late at night

rustling feverishly around the base of the house,
their long fangs clicking, their lidless eyes watching.
✡

Children's Blood

The blood of the children
Flowed out onto the street like...
Like the blood of children.

Pablo Neruda

This morning we found the bodies. I wish I could
tell you it was only a rumor and that it's

not true, but today I've seen what man can do to
one another. Sandals, ripped clothing, and mattress

springs littered the streets. In front of one house, there was
a young girl who could have been on her way to school

if she'd been in some other country. I couldn't
look at her face, or at the bulldozers' scoops, all

filled with faces. I stumbled over a doll with
curls like Sascha's. It was lying next to a pack

of cigarettes. My brand. A slender boy with a
mustache lay over the legs of a yellow-

shirted man. Their arms and legs wouldn't bend when we
gripped them. Breakfast betrayed us all. In one house, the

torn, child-swollen belly of a woman in a
red dress made us still. The television blared at

62

their uneaten dinners, congealed on the table.
Their blood cried to us from the darkened floor, and for

the first time since I've been on this trip, I was glad
you weren't with me. Outside the hospital,

one of the French photographers told me that boys
sitting on the hospital steps, boys no

older than ten or eleven, sitting on the
hospital steps the night before, staring without

flinching, had said, *Tonight we are going to die.*
He said that mothers big with unborn life had dragged

shoeless children through the streets crying, *Stop what they're
doing to us.* And boys no older than ten or

eleven saying, *Tonight they're going to kill
us.* I worked until my body cried out for rest,

then came back here to this cheap, rented room. No flares
light up tonight's darkened skies. I'm sitting here at

my desk, lighting matches between sentences to
you. I stare at the blue-edged flame, wishing it were

your sweet face. No, no faces. Not tonight. Outside,
I hear Rachel weeping for her children in the

emptied streets. Even from here, I can taste the salt
of her tears. She wants me to take her in my arms,

but I'm tired from so much weight. I light another
match, write yet another line to you, and wait. For

someone to knock
on my worn door.

Or kick it down.
Or leave me be.

Kiss Sascha,
my dear heart.

Think me
with you.

✡

Little Birds

For they have sown the wind,
and they shall reap the whirlwind.

Hosea 8:7

Little Birds

(For Rebecca Reining Keller)

Part One, 1944

Filip

One, I told them, one is all I need. They didn't
believe me, but one jerk of the trigger and the

horse was down. Before he had even discovered
evidence of our activities in the woods

behind his camp, I had shot his horse and she was
collapsing, with an outraged whinnying, beneath

him. I told them, but they wouldn't believe. He kicked
his boots frantically to free them from the stirrups,

dragged the reins away from the fall with his right hand,
extended his left arm earthward, to cushion the

jolt from my weapon. Then, cursing, pistol gleaming,
he was scrambling behind her shuddering bulk. The snow

snapped and cracked with every motion of his boots and
knees; his icy breath formed fog around his face. One,

I told them, though they have lost their faith and never
listen: one. His animal thrashed, groaned, lay still. But

what if he tries to run? I said. What if he runs
back to his camp? We'll never get him then, I said.

His own kind will protect him if he eludes us.
They said, *Yes, what if?* But he said, *No. He won't run.*

I know him, from years ago. He'll come into the
forest after us, after me. He'll go for help,

I claimed. He'll never come here searching us alone;
not if he's smart, he won't come into this forest.

And the others said, *Yes, not if he's smart.* But he
said, *No. I know him. He's a brave man. He'll come for*

us. And if we shoot his horse, he won't be faster
than we are. Yes, if we shoot his horse — we liked that —

and I have the honor. *Only the horse,* he warned,
remember, Filip. I don't forget. *Don't shoot him,*

only the horse. Not even in the leg so he
can't run back to camp? *Not even the leg only*

the horse you must remember and you must promise
do you promise? Just the horse. *How many bullets*

do you need? they asked. *How many?* One. *He might miss*
the first time, they said; *give him more.* No, I vowed, I

never miss. *But the way he is now?* they asked. *Don't*
listen to him: give him more. Mikhael's hands clenched

my shoulders to keep me with them, *No, I know that*
Filip won't miss. These extras are in case he shoots

at you after you kill his horse. He loves that horse.
Yes, he feeds her. Mischa's hands kept me still. *After*

you kill his horse, he may shoot at you. We'll give these
extra bullets to Janek so he can protect

you. Janek will guarantee that nothing happens
to Filip. But I need only one bullet. With

only one I could kill him. *Not him. Only the*
horse. Yes. And one squeeze, yes, one jerk on the trigger

and the beast he fed our vegetables was falling,
one flinch of my hand and the animal he sang

love songs and lullabies was stumbling, shrieking
while she collapsed under him. One bolt from my arm,

like I promised: he was pitched from the sky. *But what*
if he runs? we fretted. *We should at least shoot him*

in the leg. Then Mischa sighed, turning his gaunt face
toward the camp, toward the smell of those fires in the camp.

No. He won't run away, he frowned, his eyes glazed by
the memory of those belching chimneys. *He'll come.*

Marah

For intolerable minutes the frieze of the
fallen horse and its uniformed rider halted

the snow in its earthward drift, while we waited, our
weapons straining in our hands, desperate to ravage

the Kommandant. He stood, raising his lean
body like a wounded animal being taught

to re-use an injured limb. Like a dancer in
an unfamiliar part, pivoting doubtfully

with each step, he moved into the forest, pistol
readied for firing. We followed him. Some of

us scurried behind to close his path, to prevent
escape. So Filip had no reason to shoot him.

When he sagged against the tree, holding his arm, he
wasn't being a coward. He wasn't going

to give up the search. He was resting. And that's all.
He slipped the silver flask from an inside pocket to

drink, to warm himself. He wasn't abandoning
the pursuit. He was chilled and exhausted. Besides,

no matter what action the Kommandant took, we
had strict orders: under no circumstances were

we to harm him. Regardless of his crimes against
us, individually or collectively, we

were forbidden to take revenge. I'd warned Mischa
against giving Filip responsibility:

his losses have maddened him; he has become far too
eager to injure someone, anyone; he should

not have weapons. But he ignored my advice. The
Kommandant jerked as the bullet hit his left thigh,

liquor spraying from the spinning flask. Then he roared,
maneuvering over snow-covered roots, stumbling

over them. *Are you all women,* he yelled out at
us though he couldn't see us, *that you slink behind*

trees? Are you all children, he shouted from the far
side of the trunk, *that you dare not confront me?* And

then we spilled from the branches above him: all of
us, silent as snow, thinned by abuse — his abuse

in the camp — falling down on him while he shouted
beneath a cloudless sky. The force of our fall split

his lip on the bulging roots, hammered him into
the trodden snow. The idiot capered as they

tied Günther's wrists behind his back, as his
pistol was wrestled free. *Oh, please, give it to me,*

Filip pleaded, and I slapped him. *Who's not to be
trusted? Who's too anxious to injure whom?* Janek

said, grabbing the weapon and securing it at
his own belt. Filip blubbered and wept against his

arm. I twisted free, kicked bloodied snow at them. His gun
was promised to me. I held out my hand. Janek

stroked Filip's sobbing face and called me a
name, the same name they'd called me before. Then he and

Filip turned away and trudged back to where Mischa
waited for them. A few of the others heaved the

carcass of the dead horse toward our camp, to use for
food, while the others had their weapons tensed, ready

to kill the Kommandant as he had our comrades.
All around us was the tentative swirl of snow.

Filip

Let me fall, I begged them. Let me be a little
bird from barren branches; let me fall when he comes.

We need you for the horse, Mikhael said. *He who
takes the animal cannot fall.* I can, I said,

I could shoot his horse, shoot him in the leg, and fall.
Not him. What if he runs? *I know him. He won't run.*

But I saw him consider it. Yes, I saw him
think of it. On the tree of the little birds he

leaned, contemplating flight. Then he drank to mock their
thirst. Yes, they chirped, to mock us. And as he drank, he

discovered their nests; he would have caught them. *No, he
closed his eyes as he drank,* she insisted. *There was*

no reason to shoot: he didn't see us. But the
liquor, they chirped and peeped, could have opened his eyes.

He saw the little birds, I said. *Yes,* they sang. *No,*
Marah claimed, *no. You're being just like them,* she said,

full of hate. No, I swore, not little birds. *Filip
promised: only the horse.* But the silver flask, it

glinted just like a gun. *Just like one,* they sang, too.
I wanted to be a little bird to fall from

the heavens. *He disobeyed; he should be punished.*
I kept my promise, but the flash of the flask tricked

my weapon. *Just like a gun,* they peeped. Suddenly
the red was spurting through the black, and the little

birds were fluttering from the trees, so many birds
tumbling on him from the sky. He fell. They tied his

wrists so he couldn't break their wings. He gnashed his teeth
and kicked, so the birds pecked and clawed: red on black, red

on white. *We must not allow ourselves to become
like them,* Marah frowned. *We must not treat him as he*

has us. He gnashed and kicked, I said. *Yes,* they sang, *so
we pecked and clawed. Filip should be punished,* Marah

said again. But the little birds twirped, *No. No,* they
sang who fell from the sky like snow, *no. Filip kept*

*his promise, but the flask glinted like a gun; he
was protecting his little birds.* Yes, I smiled, my

little ones. *It was decided,* she said; *his fate
belongs to me,* fondling his weapon, allowing

it to rub her cheek. Let me, Marah, I begged, and
I kissed her neck, stroked her breasts through the thin dress. Let

me, Marah. Her long cool fingers on my cheek left
marks. Red on black, red on white, red on little birds.

Günther

I had despised him with such intensity for
so long that his profile, silhouetted by the

firelight, infuriated me. His voice grated
on my ears as he swaggered forward out of his

forest hideout. *I ordered only that your horse
be shot,* he said. *I told everyone that you were*

not to be harmed. As if I couldn't fight a pack
of mere women and children. I wouldn't spit on

cowards who attack a man by dropping from the
trees. Who bite, kick, scratch a man bound and unable

to defend himself. Who wrench free his weapon then
shirk from killing. Such warriors are unworthy

of the wet of my spit. They are unworthy of
disdain. But on him I spit. Him I mock with my

silence before his frenzied followers. Him I
taunt without words, surrounded by his miscreants

and sycophants. And when I discovered how those
swine had mauled my horse, plunging bits of her to cook

in the flames, I rammed into him, though my hands were
still tied behind me, roaring even after they'd

separated us, cursing till they gagged me. Late
that night, after most of them were sleeping, he came

to me and released the gag. *Don't make me kill you,*
he said. *Give in to our demands.* From where I sat,

tied to the tree, I stared at the shredded legs of
his pants. *Will you authorize an exchange?* My thigh

throbbed in rhythm with the flickering firelight. He
squatted and grabbed the collar of my uniform.

You're my hostage. You have to deal with me. The scar
I'd cut under his right eye three years earlier

glowed white. I imagined the scar I'd gouge under
the other. I won't bargain with the savage who

murdered my brother. He grew pale, shook, and staggered
away from me. A few of his warriors cried

out in dreams. I leaned my head back against the tree,
my wrists struggling to free themselves. He's a fool. And

what a mistake he made
in forbidding my death.

Mikhael

After he nodded in dozing, she crept to him,
her long fingers brushing his cheek lovingly. He

jerked away, bracing for an assault, then stared at
her shaved head. She pressed a crude cup, fashioned from a

salvaged food tin, to his lips, and urged him to drink.
The water splashed him. She knelt beside him. Her blade

sliced his pants leg, exposing the wound. He winced as
she scraped and bandaged, but didn't cry out. When she

finished, she wiped the blade on the discarded gag.
His lips moved, but I couldn't hear what he whispered.

He watched her until I marched over to the tree,
wearing his boots, kicked his legs out of my way, and

retrieved the abandoned cup. On the women's side
of the camp she was making bandages. I stood

between her and the light. When she glanced up, she flinched
at the sight of me, so I tossed the warped tin cup

into her lap and waited. Without a sound, she
pocketed the cup, bent her head over the torn

material, and began tearing and folding
again. I stomped back to the Kommandant, kicked the

snow around his thigh until I found the blood-stained
gag, tightening it in his mouth until the wound

on his lip, stretched taut, bled anew. With both hands I
seized his short-cropped hair, yanked back his head, and leaned close

to his upturned face. His eyes defied me. My breath
hung in the air between us. She didn't come back

to him that night. I did
not sleep for the watching.

Part Two, 1942

Josef

For the third time that night the captive rejected
the offered confession, refused to expose the

felons who had assaulted and murdered the new
Kommandant's brother. When I yelled, Sign it, he just

choked blood or closed his eyes. I cuffed his face until
my palm tingled, then sat to have a cigarette,

tilting my chair on its hind legs, thudding my heels
on the table's wood top. Just then the Kommandant

entered. My chair fell behind me as I jumped to
my feet. He glanced at the unsigned confession, then

asked, *Do you have anything to add?* I held my
pen above the document, but the prisoner

only glared at us. The Kommandant slid one of
my cigarettes from the package lying on the

table. *I believe we've discovered several of
your accomplices.* My match lit his cigarette.

He inhaled, blew smoke at the prisoner. *They will,
of course, receive identical punishment.* The

prisoner said nothing. *Josef,* he said, and I
picked up the pen to write additional

names: *Filip Gerhardt. Janek Müller.* The beaten
man screamed, leapt from his chair, his fists flailing while I

fumbled for my pistol, but the Kommandant had
already pinned the weeping man to the wall, bent

elbow at his throat. He snapped his fingers; I passed
the papers. *Sign,* he breathed, and the boy's tears blotted

his scribbled name. Then he hid his face behind his
hands. The confession was folded and pocketed.

For all three: deportation, on the morning train.
The prisoner shouted the Kommandant's name, but

to no avail. *Günther, you bastard,* he shouted.
Did you think we weren't lovers? The Kommandant paused,

his eyes narrowed, his jaw clenched. *You weren't her first love.
She's why you hate me,* the boy said, *why your brother*

plagued me. And then the Kommandant charged, slamming the
other into the wall. *I had her first,* the boy

spat, as their bodies scattered table, chairs. *Liar.*
he said, his service dagger flashing, slashing air,

cutting a quarter moon under the prisoner's
right eye. *I won't kill you, Mischa,* the Kommandant

panted. *I want you to suffer. Every day left
of your miserable life I want the thought of her*

in my arms to torture you. The Kommandant freed
the other one and straightened his black uniform.

The sobbing body crumpled to the floor: *she's a
Jew.* The Kommandant shook. *Think of that when you love*

her, Günther, and I'll be avenged. The door shuddered
at the officer's leaving. The bloodied boy howled.

I kicked the door open:
the cell stank of stale smoke.

Mikhael

Ju-de, he chanted as I rounded the corner,
sack of food close to my body. *Ju-de,* he hissed.

Leave me alone, Wilhelm. He wrenched me around to
face him. *I hear you went to her house yesterday.*

His fingers danced on his weapon. I shifted the
sack, sighed loudly, crossed the street. He lurched into me,

his baton butting my chest. *She's my brother's girl.*
The stick's pressure persuaded me to step back. Just

go away, Wilhelm. *Not until you abandon
all hope of reclaiming her.* I retreated once

more. Is your brother becoming nervous? He laughed,
thudded my arm. *She wouldn't have anything to*

do with you, Parasite. He whacked the groceries.
Consider this warning a favor. Stay away

from his woman. The bag ripped. Tomatoes splattered.
Cabbages leapt into the street. His eyes glinted.

Forbidden food, he growled, cracking my collarbone.
I shoved him against the building, lapels crushed to

his cheeks. *My brother will finish you,* he sputtered.
She had exchanged me for Günther, and there, against

the dulled red of brick, Wilhelm's blond hair became his
brother's. Bastard. I bashed Günther's face into the

stone until, pulpy and stilled, it shimmered into
the grin of his younger brother, eyes fixed. Wilhelm?

His body slid down the rough wall. Wilhelm? I slipped
on the dropped baton, scraping my wrists and hands, my

identification card and ration coupons
scattering. *Ju-de. Judenrein.* As I ran, their

fetters snarled and tangled
around my pounding heels.

Josef

Her light hair was tousled and her blue eyes swollen
when she arrived, requesting the Kommandant by

first name. I informed her that he was out. She paused,
darted behind me, flung open his office door.

Fräulein, I protested. *Marah,* the Kommandant
was startled into standing. *He told me you weren't*

here, she glared at me. The Kommandant corrected.
Obviously a mistake, Josef, since, as you

can see, I am in. Jawohl, Herr Kommandant. I
saluted rigidly. *Günther, my family needs*

our help. He yanked his hand free of hers, gazed out the
windows. *I can be of no service, Fräulein.* She

stared, open-mouthed. He tapped his baton on his palm.
She slipped between him and the windowpane. *Günther,*

she said, *what are you doing?* She gasped as he jerked
away, strode from her. *I'm very busy, Fräulein.*

The Kommandant lit a cigarette. *They've taken
my Uncle Meier, and Mischa's been arrested.*

We must help them. He sat down at his desk. *There's
nothing I can do.* He put out his cigarette

and rummaged through some papers piled on his desk. She
stood there, her fingers at her throat. *What do you mean,*

there's nothing you can do? Exactly that, he said.
His pen scratched loudly on the papers as he signed

his name. She rushed forward and captured his hand with
hers. *I know you resent my past with another,*

but my uncle… Don't do this, she wept. *Don't destroy
our relationship.* He roared, getting to his feet,

pushing her aside as he reached for a folder,
pulling out the ancestry inquiry. *How*

dare you? he choked hoarsely, revealing the scarlet
J which was stamped beside her picture. *Who betrayed*

whom? he said, throwing the folder across the room.
Her fingers covered her mouth. *But you must have known:*

I don't hide it. He walked away from her. *Günther,*
she said. *I thought we loved each other. Never,* he

said, grabbing and shaking her, *I never loved you.*
When he released her she fell against the wall. He

smoothed his jacket and hair. *Josef.* I clicked my heels.
I am not in. Jawohl. *To anyone.* She fled

the room while I retrieved the scattered papers. He
waved me impatiently away. I saluted,

exited, then realized I still held her file.
I opened the door to return it: his shoulders

shuddered convulsively; his hands wrenched his hair. Back
at my desk, I took a deportation order

from my drawer, printed the name I found beneath her
photograph, painstakingly traced the Kommandant's

signature from a letter. I glanced at his closed
door. The wastebasket swallowed her folder's contents.

His muffled moans accompanied the *snick* and flare
of my matches. Then I dropped them in. To free him.

Filip

Today, I warned, but they were scrounging potato
peels by the kitchen door. Today, I prophesied,

but they were scavenging for scraps of bread under
the sawdust mattresses. He's been sent to fight our

comrades, I revealed, but they were organizing
cigarettes. They never listen. At noon we were

confined to quarters. *What's happening?* they worried,
as the chimneys ceased their smoking. *What's happening?*

they fretted, as the silver buttons on the guards'
uniforms gleamed expectantly. He's coming, I

fidgeted, and they crowded behind me at the
window. *Who?* they asked me. The sleek car crept through the

gates. They never listen. The rear door opened, and
black boots planted gracefully in the muddied red

clay turned into him: the Death's-Header. At last, I
said. He's here. *Who is it?* they whispered behind me,

and they shivered, clutching at my threadbare sleeves. His
profile, haloed by the sun behind him, nodded

at the practiced salutes of the guards. *Who is he?*
they asked, plucking at my worn sleeves and trousers. *Are*

you Filip Gerhardt? the police had questioned me,
then pinned my arms behind. *Papa, Papa,* my twins

had cried as the dark uniforms elevated
them. *You're under arrest.* Police had thumped me down

the stairs. *Filip,* my wife Anya had called, until
their weapons silenced her. The rifles and pistols

paraded the camp's new Kommandant. I know you.
In the cell, Janek had been cradling Mischa; my

fingers had touched their wet faces: *what have we done?*
The prison door had clanked against the stone wall, and

his ashen hair had glowed with the hall's weak light. We
had gazed, trembling, up at him. The pallor of his

hair had loomed over the huddled three of us: I
memorized him. *This is our horse-keeper,* the guards

informed the Kommandant. His eyes flashed. *What are you
called?* he asked, slicing an apple, slipping the moist

piece to his tongue from the knife. *He never speaks sense,*
the guards confided, prodding me, *but he loves the*

horses. The Kommandant nodded, chewing. *Then you
shall stay,* he addressed me, lifting my chin with the

flat of the blade. *And thou shalt be called Horse-Lover.*
His boys snorted with laughter. I stared at him. He

smiled. *You remind me of someone,* he said as his
tongue caught another slice. I glanced down while he chewed.

My horse is Hilda. I nodded. *You sleep in here
with her.* Yes. But when my comrades beckoned, I ran.

Dirt clods leapt at my eyes and mouth. Forest branches
snagged my arms and face. Gnarled roots threatened to trip me.

Mischa, I shouted, tangled in the undergrowth.
The partisans separated themselves from the

trees. Mischa, I cried, until his hands on my face
saved me. *Filip,* he hugged me. *How did you find us?*

Mischa, I said, pointing
toward the camp. He's come.

Part Three, 1944

Marah

For three days and nights snow obliterated the
horizon, while allied and enemy shells clashed

with relentless thundering beyond the blinding
veil of white. Three days the Kommandant rejected

opportunities to ransom himself, refused
to permit his adjutant Josef to exchange

the commanding officer's life for our *Kazett*
comrades. Each confrontation with Mikhael brought

on determined deafness or a spiteful, stony
gaze. I understood that Mischa would not suffer

Günther's arrogance indefinitely, but I
also knew that I could approach neither of them.

Liebchen, had escaped him after I had dressed his
wound, but my tongue had cleaved to the roof of my mouth,

and snow had fallen with stifling finality.
Mischa slapped the thin soup that I was spooning to

Günther, spilling some on our captive's coat. *Someone
else will feed him,* he said, *or else he can starve.* Legs

apart, arms crossed, Mikhael stood watch until I
had extricated myself from their quarreling eyes.

Had I foreseen this captivity, I never
would have tasted the seeds of the pomegranate.

Where Lightning Strikes

The others were sleeping by the time he came to
me, towering in the greatcoat and boots. I rose.

What will we do if he won't exchange our comrades?
Mischa asked, palming the prized pistol from one hand

to the other. *How will I break him if he won't
surrender?* I ended his hands' agitated

movement by resting my fingers on the weapon,
the elegant metal stark against his fingers,

coarsened by the lifetime in the camp, in this cold.
What will you do, Mischa? My fingers stroked the warm

barrel, curved around its length. *Kill him.* I relieved
him of the pistol's weight, laid it beside my own

weapon, turned back to his haggard face: burden me
with the duty. *Liebeleh,* he struggled, his voice

hoarse and wondering as that of a lost child, found.
My fingertips against his chapped lips ended his

words, and his breath warmed my skin, long accustomed to
the chill of loneliness and survival. He stretched

his hand to trace, without touching, the line of my
cheek and collarbone; the swell of my breasts made him

pause. I kissed him with the kisses of my mouth; my
ribs shuddered under the warmth of his hesitant

palms. He lowered himself till he knelt before me.
My touch melted the ice fragments tangled in his

short curls, and my fingers plunged behind the collar
at the nape of his neck. All around us, sleepers

breathed the song of those who had fallen, but he did
not dwell on former things, nor did I remind him.

Filip

Don't ignore me, I told her, trailing behind as
she gathered broken branches for the fires; let me

do it. She forced another armload into my
makeshift pack, without answering. Each time she bent,

the tender twigs leapt to her warm hands, crackled at
her touch. I have experience, I said, stroking

the Kommandant's gun; her fingers cracked cold against
my cheek. But she didn't slap him, and he went to

her without permission. She stood as the wind caught
the plundered greatcoat, billowing it behind him.

Liebeleh. She grasped the coat's lapels, dragging him
close, her mouth open on his. Be my little bird,

I crooned in her ear, yet her weapon's muzzle pressed
into my side until I was forced to retreat,

until I flew, grumbling, to our prisoner, whose
wound she nursed, though she had been forbidden to do

so, whom she fed soup and brown bread when Mischa was
not near, despite repeated warnings and threats. When

Mischa promised love she didn't shove a pistol
at his belly. I'm the one to do it, I swore,

and her hands' force toppled me backwards into the
trees' roots, splintering my sack's kindling. She didn't

86

push him away. Her long fingers wove themselves in
his hair, crushed him to her. Afterward, she rose, gazed

at his slumbering form. Then she and the weapon
hovered over the sleeping officer, but her

hands held no bandages, and I had already
organized the last crust of bread. Eventually,

she eased herself to sitting, her back against my
tree, between them. With her head on the bark, she stared

at a starless sky. I approached, knelt beside her,
but she stayed still. I edged closer, laid my head on

her shoulder. She didn't move. Filip loves Marah,
I whispered, so her strong arms would encircle me.

Poor little one, she cooed, and, safe in her arms at
last, I dreamt of clean sheets, cabbage soup, caraway.

Günther

Just before dawn I saw the idiot and his
mute companion rouse their fearless leader, who scowled

and grimaced at the half-wit's gesticulations.
During the ensuing conference with the girl, the

imbecile perched on his haunches in front of me,
sighting me down his pistol. I should have ordered

his execution when I first detected the
ammunition shortages. He was not quite the

cretin he feigned. Do it, Horse-Lover, I said, but
he ran to Mischa. When my pistol was deposited in

Marah's hands, the simpleton argued, shaking his
head, pointing to his own chest, but Marah wouldn't

relinquish it. Mischa's protégés swarmed around,
heaping their bodies with stolen weaponry, and

disappeared, one by one, into the deafening
snowstorm. Soon, only the fool, his mute, and the girl

remained. Their leader, in confiscated boots and
coat, directed them to me. The oaf danced in an

erratic circle around Marah. *It seems all*
negotiations have been suspended, Mischa

smiled wryly. *Your camp has been liberated by*
the advancing front. The half-wit hopped from one foot

to the other. *Please let me do it,* he said. *Your*
brave soldiers have deserted their posts, Mischa scoffed,

so we no longer need a hostage. I stared at
him silently. *Let me do him,* the fool said as

Marah readied my weapon: snap and click. *I'll meet*
you there, she told them, aiming steadily at me.

Do it quickly, Mischa suggested, as the three
of them vanished into the swirling cold. Snowflakes

dissolved on her pallid face, on her long, dusky
lashes. Liebling, I protested, but her finger

jerked twice on the trigger, splaying bark on either
side of my face. My eyes opened. The boots that were

slung over her shoulder, she dashed at my feet. In
her hand, my service dagger cut the bonds that held

my wrists, cut those that shackled me. Marah, I caught
the wrist that freed me. It's imperative that I

have a weapon. *No, you're the enemy.* I leaned
forward. I'm Günther, I said. The knife's blade opened

the left chest of my uniform. I glanced down: the
fingers wrapped around the dagger's handle uncurled

and I took it. Her fingers brushed my unshaved
cheek. Then she, too, shimmered into the whirling white.

Marah

For days after we had finally ambushed the
Kommandant, Filip alternated between threats

and admonishments in his desperation to
convince Mikhael that Filip himself was the

only viable and trustworthy candidate
to execute our collective revenge. For months,

a moth irresistibly drawn toward yet fleeing
the inferno of an irrevocable choice,

Mischa had vacillated between his need to
avenge his own mistreatment and his desire for

evidence that I was not captive to the past.
His eyes, when they gazed at mine, sought assurance that

my perception of our fate and obligation
was indistinguishable from his. As long as

the German pistol was in my hands when we fled,
it mattered not his reason for assigning me

the awful task. Filip stammered objections to
no effect: the prize was indisputably mine.

Do it before he convinces you otherwise,
Mischa cautioned, from the far side of our sorrows.

Günther returned the muzzle's stare unblinkingly.
I sought you, he confessed, and the bark beside his

face splattered, *but I found you not.* I flung him the
boots, cut away the ropes. He seized my wrist and yanked

forward with such force that the blade pierced the jacket.
I am not your enemy. I allowed him to

pry free the dagger, but my wrist beat against the
bars of his fingers when he pulled my hand to his

face. *Liebling.* His rough lips and cheek chafed my emptied
palm. Then my feet were plodding through the mounting snow,

and Filip's face loomed out of the surrounding white.
Is it done? he said, with doubting eyes. Run, I warned,

grabbing his hand, dragging him, stumbling, after me.
Our hearts pounded in our numbed ears, and the shells that

betokened freedom crashed
in the air above us.

Filip

You're next, my pistol and I promised him. He spat
at the snow at my feet, yawned when I lowered the

weapon to see him better. *Do it, Fool,* he said.
I hurried to Mischa to demand permission.

90

No. The promises she had wrested from him in
the dark bound him still, so the right to exact our

revenge was hers. None should escape or remain, I
warned, and her ears seemed to catch my cry. Her own voice

had sounded with ours, and she had sworn that she no
longer loved him. Yet she emerged from the white snow

with moist eyes and damp cheeks. It isn't done, I said,
my pistol prepared to force her return, but the

momentum of her flight swallowed my outrage. *Come,*
she chanted, *come,* and in my desire to maintain

my grip on her slender fingers, my indignant
words were lost in the rushing wind. At the point of

rendezvous, she nodded in response to Mischa's
raised eyebrows. I grunted protest, but her look quelled

revelations. Mischa indicated our new
destination, and we scattered, in smaller groups.

Janek and I flew with him. At our first rest, I
attempted disclosure, but then the sky opened:

two in uniform were suddenly upon us.
Grunt, snap, crack: the two Germans lay stilled. She faltered

at the crucial moment. *Not now, Filip.* The train's
clanking and more guttural shouts penetrated

the woods. *Quick: Into their uniforms,* Mischa urged.
Janek's broad back and shoulders struggled vainly to

squeeze into either of the narrow jackets. *We'll
find another,* Mischa stated, donning one of

the Death's-Headers' caps. I should have been the one to…
Not now. Mischa handed me one of their daggers:

Mehr sein als scheinen. At the halted train, Mischa
and I mingled among other uniforms. My

heart fluttered in its disguise. We should have killed him
while we had the chance. *Shhh,* Mischa cautioned. We found

an empty cattle car, scraped the wood door closed. When
the train lurched forward, we opened the door, motioned

to Janek to join us, our hands and arms stretched out
to capture his, catching him, pulling, straining till

he stood beside us in the empty cattle car.
Once inside, we embraced and kissed each other. Our

hands trembling despite the black uniforms. With one
I could have done it, I said. One. *Please, Filip.* With

a prolonged metallic moan the train paused again
and several disheveled uniforms crammed into

our car. Mischa shoved Janek back, leveled his gun
at him, hushed me with his wide eyes. *Ein Jude,* the

others snarled, pointing, beckoning to one whose bright hair
blinded the three of us. Mischa swallowed. I flinched.

Janek's white-knuckled fists clenched, unclenched, clenched, and our
captured Kommandant's eyes blazed fierce and vibrant blue.

Mikhael

Justice is not inflicting suffering, she said
as I bit into the potato, chewed the charred

92

skin. *Filip will torture him.* Persuade me that you
deserve revenge more than he, I said, eating, and

she stomped away. In the end, the weapon tugged toward
her outstretched hand, so I let it be: I had to

concern myself with our swift and safe dispersal.
Filip continued to debate my decision.

Be still, I snapped. He sulked several paces behind,
and when she rejoined us, he growled disapproval.

We ran until our hearts' thumping bent us over,
gasping. I ignored his renewed complaints, almost

missed the warning *snap click* of a readied weapon,
the German's hiss to his partner: *Josef. Juden.*

Neither of the dispatched Germans' uniforms would
fit Janek, and his eyes rounded, his breath quickened.

Don't worry, I said, to calm him. *She failed us,* said
Filip, and I shouted at him, Not now. His lip

quivered and his eyes filled with tears. I settled the
cap on his head, placed my palm against his cheek. First

we must save ourselves. Then we'll see to him. Mutely,
he nodded. I nudged the uniformed Filip through

the throng of guards, deposited him in the train's
car, then returned to rescue Janek. When the train

screeched to a halt, Filip moaned, and though I tried to
shield Janek from the Germans' view, they saw him right

away. They grumbled and growled at the sight of him,
then divided themselves to make a path for the

one of highest rank. Günther strode forward, his eyes
bludgeoning the air from my chest. His bullet's force

drove Janek's body into the back wall. *Ja,* the
others smiled. *You,* he shouted at me. *You,* he barked,

signaling Filip. *Pick it up. Get it out of
here.* He herded the others aside. *Not one of*

them shall survive us. The Germans growled agreement.
I leapt down from the car, accepted the body's

weight, was joined by a quaking Filip. *Find yourselves
another place,* Günther tugged at the massive door;

*this has just been designated an officers'
car.* His cronies murmured agreement. Filip and

I crouched over Janek, gazed up at the train as
it yanked away. Günther looked down at us as he

dragged the warped and splintered door, in slowed motion, closed.
At the very last instant, he raised his hand. The

train slid away from us. Lifting Janek's heels and
shoulders, Filip and I carried him to the trees,

collapsing beyond the sight of the train. Weeping,
Filip sat on his heels, rocked back and forth, cradling

Janek's head in his lap. The train's whistle lowed, a
slow mournful drone, and Filip's heaving sobs were but

a surrogate for the
cries trapped in my own throat.

Where Lightning Strikes

Günther

I encountered the others sooner than I had
anticipated, was infuriated by

their unkempt demeanor. My raving expletives
restored discipline. They jerked to stiff attention:

Jawohl, Herr Kommandant. We departed for their
original destination. Snow dazed us

and bursting shells deafened us to the approach of
partisans, who were alone or in groups of three.

We defeated many, but their unexpected
appearances caused the loss of several of my

own men. We were eventually joined by others:
army men, including officers, though none of

a higher rank. They saluted me rigidly.
Most of the train's cars stank, and we searched until we

located one that was slightly less filthy. We
were barely aboard when some commotion began,

with shouts of *Jude.* The others parted, and there:
Mischa and his Horse-Lover, desecrating our

uniform, and the mute, cowering behind them.
Before they could reveal my own ignominy,

I silenced the hulking one, ordered the others
off the train. My comrades did not interfere. The

train's departure meant their abandonment: Mischa
glared at me. For a moment, I considered some

motion or gesture, to make him understand my
own fear and desperation, but the look on his

face stopped me. Besides, I knew it was futile to
explain anything to him: she might understand

my behavior and forgive me, but he was too
infested with anger and envy and hate to

be empathetic. I let the door slam. The train's
vibrations and my oozing wound nauseated

me. Sweat accumulated on my upper lip
and forehead. My temples throbbed. I lowered myself

into the mangy stray in the far corner, mopped
my face with a dirty handkerchief, massaged my

neck, and fingered the borrowed weapon. Through the
night, the train's swaying rocked me, but not to dreaming.

Marah

For half a day beyond the designated time
of meeting, the others waited with me, their eyes

darting like imprisoned animals endlessly
pacing the cage's space, hoping to discover

some overlooked escape route. For tense hours, they peered
anxiously into the vast blank snow, looking for

signs of Mischa and the others, debating the
safety of so many of us staying in one

place for such a long time, arguing and pleading
for my leadership on the perilous journey

still ahead of us, echoed Mischa's parting words:
Save yourselves. Finally, as it grew darker, all but

two of them abandoned me. I should have bid the
rest of them farewell, or commended them to God's

protection, but I was concentrating on the
immense, impenetrable fog of snow for clues

of Mischa's impending arrival. I didn't
watch their leaving. I nodded at the sound of their

apologetic voices, and reluctantly
bore their departing touches on my shoulder, but

it meant nothing to me. Even their leaving some
additional ammunition and rations of

bread crusts at my side didn't convince me of their
loyalty. I couldn't condone their deliberate

desertion of Mischa, even if it was one
that he had anticipated — no, expected — should

he fail to appear at the appointed hour and
designated place. How could they abandon him?

Hadn't he rescued them, kept them alive, turned them
into warriors? Yet, now, amnesiac, they

considered only themselves. When I finally turned
around from my post, my blurred eyes found the two whose

fidelity exceeded their fear. My brief tears
acknowledged their loyalty. They nodded dumbly,

divided the food and bullets into thirds, shrugged
at my attempted expressions of gratitude.

I returned to my vigil. By dawn, two shadowed
figures in uniform limped toward us. My rifle

raised. *Neyn,* Mischa's voice sounded over the storm, while
Filip's red-rimmed eyes revealed Janek's fate. Mischa

hardly glanced at the three of us as he trudged in
the direction of the border. Filip's sniffles

were woven into the fabric of our breathing,
while ahead, an aloof beacon, Mischa's silence

threatened to unravel
even the blameless snow.

Mikhael

Only after he had severed the six-pointed
gold star from the shirt's left breast, after we had heaped

snow and fashioned it, with our hot tears, into a
glistening mound, after we had chanted, *Oh, let*

His great Name be blessed forever and throughout all
eternity, only then could I overcome

Filip's resolution to remain with Janek.
He kissed the frayed yellow patch, then slipped it inside

his shirt, against his bare skin. I glanced away each
time Filip stroked it, sighing, convincing himself

of its safety. As soon as I perceived her gun's
sighting us, I shrilled "No" in the language that she

would most quickly recognize. Her weapon lowered.
I swept by her without uttering another

syllable. We ran without talk, our steaming breath
hovering, drifting past our faces as we moved,

our feet chuffing like the metal womb we pursued.
The train's engine was just derailing, at the tracks

our fellows had blasted near the border, by the
time we stragglers managed to overtake it. My

comrades assaulted me with hugs, kisses, backslaps.
We yanked open the train's doors, one by one, and yelled

Raus, Raus, to the Germans hunched inside. They tumbled
out, dumbfounded. We shot all of them, except one,

as they were attempting to escape. Left alone,
Günther turned his weapon's handle and offered me

the gun, saluting, clicking his heels together:
Sieg heil. When he raised his hands above his head, he

grinned at me, and the crack of my knuckles as they
collided with his jawbone pleased me immensely.

I spat on him where he lay, sprawled in the dirtied
snow at my feet. *We'll have to take him with us.* I

turned to Marah, gently stroked her wind-burnt cheek. First
we have to transform Günther into one of us.

We'll need the others to hold him down securely.
I shoved the two guns behind my belt. Filip, you

have my permission to kill him if he attempts
escape. *Yes, sir.* His gun gouged the German's temple.

What the hell are you planning? And, Filip, shoot him
if he speaks: I don't want to hear the sound of his

voice. *Oh, thank you, Mischa.* Marah touched my arm, *Will
you get the others, or shall I? We can't remain*

here long. Yes, I know. You belong to me, Günther,
I warned, then ran, smiling, to fetch my strongest men.

Marah

For as long as he could maintain, in the whipping
wind, the pose of triumphant conquistador, legs

wide, fists on hips, Mischa towered, smirking, over
the felled Kommandant. Then he spat on him, like some

insolent bully, dominating the schoolyard.
I turned away. *Kill him if he so much as makes*

a sound, he instructed his eager disciple,
relishing the role of victor. For the next few

minutes Filip taunted Günther, imitating
Mikhael the Tyrant. *If he sneezes, I can*

shoot him, Filip ruminated, the weapon wedged
tightly against Günther's temple and cheek. Leave him

be, I ordered, rummaging through Günther's jacket
pockets until I discovered three cigarettes

and a small container of matches. Besides, he
didn't tell you to torment the Kommandant, did

he? I said as I passed him one of the lighted
cigarettes. After I had breathed in some of the

second cigarette, I placed it to Günther's lips.
Marah, Filip sputtered and choked, *that's not right.* Why?

100

Mischa didn't tell you to shoot him for breathing.
Filip frowned and squatted on his haunches, sucking

the contraband cigarette as if he were an
infant, finally locating the withheld breast. Each

time I leaned near, Günther's hand brushed my knee, and his
blue eyes closed as the smoke rushed into his lungs. *It*

just doesn't seem fair, Filip complained. Nothing does
anymore, I said. When Mischa returned to us,

I offered him the remaining cigarette. He
smiled as he stroked my cheek and murmured, *Liebeleh.*

The others surrounded Günther, hauled him to his
feet and shoved him toward the safe-house. The Kommandant

didn't resist their rough movements. Inside the safe-
house, the bent grey farmer gaped and trembled when he

saw that we had captured a German officer,
but he said nothing. Amidst numerous curses

and countless unwarranted blows, the Kommandant
was stripped of his fine uniform and dressed in a

prisoner's rags. Günther submitted to all these
indignities in silence. Then Mischa signaled

the farmer, who hesitantly shuffled nearer,
bearing a small tray with various instruments.

The boys forced the Kommandant's left sleeve up. Günther
glanced at the needle uncomprehendingly till

they held out his inner left forearm for marking.
Nein, he shouted, kicking and struggling violently

toppling the chair and several of his captors. *Nein.*
Mischa's cocked gun coerced him into submission.

Resettled, weighted by bodies, Günther panted
through clenched teeth, his eyes narrowed with the agony

of that latest humiliation. Afterward,
though he was liberated from their binding hands,

he sat slumped in the broken chair, staring at the
scuffed wooden floor. Mischa stood and delivered to

my hand the coveted service dagger: *Meine Ehre*
heisst Treue. I approached Günther. He didn't look

up, even after I placed my hand on his head.
Then suddenly, he breathed, *Marah,* too faintly for

any of their ears to catch. The farmer watched in
amazement. The sun's light glinted on the dancing

blade, and Günther's hair, curled
around my fingers, fell.

Filip

Now is our enemy, who has slain many of
us, delivered into our hands, I rejoiced, as

the farmer's needle pricked Janek's numbers onto
the Kommandant's forearm, blue-black on the forearm

of our enemy, the symbol of our shame and
our triumph. At last is the destroyer of our

country taken, I said, embracing each of my
comrades, who patted me on the back, smiling. *Yes,*

Filip, they said. *We've won at last.* Then the farmer
dutifully made the needle comply with Mischa's

other request: on either side of the numbers,
he tattooed a six-pointed star. Our six-pointed

star. The Kommandant gritted his teeth throughout the
marking, glaring viciously at Mischa, but when

it was all finished, he collapsed in the chair. That's
when Marah went to him, the bright dagger flashing.

At long last the enemy of our people is
delivered into our hands, I said. And this time

he shall not escape. In the forest, we had bound
him, hand and foot, with new ropes, never used, yet he

had flung those from him as if they had been mere flies.
Marah hiked her skirt up above her knees and stood

over the seated Kommandant so that her legs,
bare and pale, confined his, her bare thighs taut around

his. She grasped his hair. We tensed. His lips moved, but we
could not hear his whisperings. With steady strokes the

blade slashed his ashen hair, shimmering in the sun's
light. With each tug of her long slender fingers, with

each sigh of the slicing steel, the Kommandant, eyes
closed, lips parted, breathed warm upon her breasts. His legs

strained between hers, and his curls, representative
Aryan wisps, shuddered over her wrists, across

his shoulders, onto the bared floor. Now his strength is
gone, I assured Mischa, touching his arm, and he

is just like any other man. *Sieg heil,* Mischa
murmured, averting his eyes, lighting the final

cigarette. Marah eased herself away from the
cropped Kommandant, crossed the room to Mischa. *It's done,*

she sighed, and shook the German's hair from her hands, brushed
it from her wrinkled dress. Mischa inhaled, released

smoke in disintegrating circles. The branded
Kommandant examined the blue-black scratchings. The

farmer swept the shavings
into a pile. *It's done.*

Günther

By the time I realized how they intended to
maim me, by scraping the dead one's identity

into my skin, there was nothing to be done to
prevent it. Their mass overpowered my resistance,

mocked my failure to determine my fate at my
own hands. The pain of this defeat stunned me, and my

body capitulated. Her hand on my head
recalled me to myself, and I spoke her name. *Shhh.*

Each time she bent my head, freeing my scalp of some
of its weight, I shut my eyes, inhaled her body's

warmth. When she finished, she turned the weapon over
to Mischa, as I had earlier surrendered

the other. He said nothing. The old man bustled
about, coughing nervously. I could not consume

the food he presented, and sat in the corner,
staring at the marks blackening my forearm. *You*

need to eat something, to maintain your strength, Marah
spoke softly, offering the plate again. *We still*

have an arduous journey ahead. I wished to
accept the nourishment, to graze her hand with mine

at the passing of the plate, to tell her things I
had done that were best forgotten. But the loathsome

words disgorged themselves as incomprehensible
sounds, and I turned my face from her, so she could not

witness my cowardice and my shame. She touched the
back of my head. I swallowed my remaining doubts.

Marah, I whispered, but her fingers against my
lips prevented my confession. *Eat.* Early the

next morning, rough kicks ended my fitful sleep, and
their movement hustled me outside. *You're coming with*

us, Mischa stated, frowning at the horizon.
Marah and the Horse-Lover flanked him. *If you run*

fast enough, you'll live. What? The idiot flashed his
gun: *I'll be right behind.* I prefer to face my

executioners, rather than be shot in the
back, as a coward. *We're not Germans,* Mischa spat.

We should have turned you into smoke in the chimneys,
the fool growled, swaggering forward. *Run, and don't look*

back. I don't trust you. *It doesn't matter, because*
you either run, or die. Mischa smiled, cocking his

own weapon. *Günther,* Marah's voice came to me, *run.*
I ran. The idiot's chuckling chased me, until

my own breath sounded in my ears. I longed to turn
to see if she, at least, were with me, but dared not,

lest hatred destroy me. I had bungled my last
opportunity for heroics. I had failed

to earn her forgiveness. I had been betrayed. I
ran, and ran, and ran. The cold was all around me.
✡

About Alexandria

Alexandria Constantinova Szeman

Critically acclaimed & award-winning author, Alexandria Constantinova Szeman (formerly writing as "Sherri" Szeman because her 1st editor told her that her name "wouldn't fit on the book cover," & wanted an "easy" first name to go with her "hard" last name) began as a poet before she started writing novels, short fiction, and creative writing books.

Szeman has Ph.D.'s in Creative Writing and in English & Comparative World Literatures. Her dissertation, *Survivor: One Who Survives* (University of Cincinnati, 1986) was a collection of original poetry, all of which were accepted or published by university & literary journals before her dissertation defense. While in graduate school, her poetry was awarded numerous prizes, including The Elliston Poetry Prize (several times) & The Isabel and Mary Neff Creative Writing Fellowship.

Her first novel, *The Kommandant's Mistress,* on the Holocaust from multiple points of view and perspectives, was chosen as one of *The New York Times Book Review*'s "Top 100 Books of the Year" (1993). It was also awarded the University of Rochester's (NY) prestigious Kafka Prize "for the outstanding book of prose fiction by an American woman" (1994), and Central State University's (OH) Talmadge McKinney Research Award (1993).

Originally published by HarperCollins (1993) & HarperPerennial (1994), the novel has been sold to publishers in 10 foreign countries and translated into French, Spanish, Russian, Lithuanian, Danish, Swedish, Norwegian, among others. It was republished by Arcade (2000) & was optioned for film (though funded, it was never made).

Her second novel, *Only with the Heart,* on the devastating effects of Alzheimer's on a family, is on the recommended reading lists of Alzheimer's Associations nationwide. Originally published by Arcade (2000), the Revised & Expanded, 12th Anniversary Edition contains new scenes with updated medical treatment/medications for Alzheimer's, as well as new legal definitions and statutes regarding assisted suicide.

Her third novel, *No Feet in Heaven,* about two brothers and their female cousin who decide to attain fame by hunting down a notorious serial killer themselves, won praise from several NY editors before it was accepted by a New York Trade House; unfortunately, that House was purchased by a larger NY Trade House: the editor was then laid off, and the book "rejected."

The titular story in her award-winning collection of short stories, *Naked, with Glasses,* won Third Prize in *Story Magazine*'s "Seven Deadly Sins Contest" (1995), and the manuscript won the Grand

Prize in the UKA Press [United Kingdom Authors Press] 2007 Annual International Writing Competition.

Her two poetry collections, *Love in the Time of Dinosaurs* and *Where Lightning Strikes: Poems on the Holocaust,* both contain critically acclaimed & award-winning poems. Each volume includes several poems from her dissertation, *Survivor: One Who Survives* (University of Cincinnati, 1986). The poems have won several prizes, including University of Cincinnati's Elliston Prize (anonymous competition; 1983, 1984, 1985), an Honorable Mention in the Chester H. Jones Poetry Foundation National Poetry Competition (1985), Michigan State University's *The Centennial Review* Michael Miller Award for Poetry (1985), an Honorable Mention in *Writer's Digest* National Writing Competition (1980), and The Isabel & Mary Neff Fellowship for Creative Writing (1984-85). Both volumes were unanimously accepted for publication by all outside readers of UKA Press [United Kingdom Authors Press] in 2004.

Szeman is currently completing her latest novel, as well as revising her memoir (about growing up with a mother who practiced Munchausen's by Proxy), and is about to publish several creative writing exercise books, including an updated version of her classic *Mastering Point of View* (originally published by Story Press, 2001).

Alexandria's Amazon Author Central Page
Amazon.com/author/alexandriaszeman

Alexandria's Web-Site
AlexandriaConstantinovaSzeman.com

Read excerpts from all her books:
AlexandriaConstantinovaSzeman.com/Books.php

Alexandria's Blog: The Alexandria Papers
TheAlexandriaPapers.com
AlexandriaConstantinovaSzeman.com/Blog.php

Alexandria's Twitter @Alexandria_SZ
Twitter.com/Alexandria_SZ
AlexandriaConstantinovaSzeman.com/Twitter.html

Contact Alexandria
AlexandriaConstantinovaSzeman.com/Contact.php